DEEP
PHOTOGRAPHS

The Education of a Sociologist

David Weiner

DEEP PHOTOGRAPHS

The Education of a Sociologist

David Weiner

Published By
Positive Imaging, LLC
http://positive-imaging.com
9016 Palace Parkway
Austin, TX 78748

ISBN: 0-9842480-6-4

LCCN: 2012930450

Acknowledgements and Dedications

This *album* is dedicated to Melanie, Hillary, and Mr. Kennedy, the vice principal. It is also dedicated to those who nurtured me, badgered me, corrected me, encouraged me, read me, edited me, and insisted I publish even if no big publishing house would take the risk. Thanks for your support and help: Claudette, the most competent, giving, and kind reader/editor a brand new writer could wish for; Arielle, Barbara, Beryl, Carl, Jessica, Leslie, Letitia, Lynn, Melanie, and my best friend and wife, Shula, who lovingly forced me to do it.

Finally, my deep gratitude to Bill Benitez. The assistance provided went far beyond what self-publishing usually implies. He has been partner, editor, mentor and dear friend. His combination of technical savvy and artistic sensitivity continue to astound me.

Preface

I believe that Plato and Kant must have been right. No one perceives reality directly. We can only observe the shadows cast by real events. These shadows flicker tauntingly–on the walls of our inner caves. We cannot resist the urge to make sense of them. Our own individual experiences are tiny events within the larger context of things. Separately, they often seem meaningless. Our experiences are not really unique phenomena, however. They are, after all, parts of the whole. Their shadows, therefore, must indicate more than our separate realities.

These are the stories of some of my significant experiences as a sociologist and educator during the last thirty some-odd years. More blown about by the winds of fate than in control of my own destiny, I have been both participant and observer of things I am still trying to understand. I think of my stories as photographs of events which are seminal, and therefore cast shadows.

I'm not certain what impels me to include only these photographs and not others. I sense that they especially reveal our hunger to connect, and the destructive ideologies that urge our alienation. If the implications of my stories are not always pleasant, they only reflect essential qualities of our society.

I suspect that most people will find themselves and their own experiences within this "album".

Contents

Part 1: **L. A. County**

Indian Wrestling 9

Motivation 17

The Solar System 22

Parents 26

Sunflower Seeds 28

James Meredith 29

Melanie 33

The Vice Principal 39

Part 2: **The Bay Area**

Hillary 43

The Petition 50

The Meensom Boys 56

Part 3: **Graduate School**

Sociology 63

Love 69

Shula 72

Intergroup Relations 81

Freshmen 89

Part 4:   **Up East**

Social Work   97

Police   106

Foremen   111

Part 5:   **Back Home**

Jack   119

Existential Sociology   132

The Student With Connections   140

Civil Engineering   147

Expulsion   155

Part 6:   **The "Real" World**

Training and Recruiting   159

Hatchet Work   170

Part 7:   **The Middle East**

Russians   181

Bedouins   189

Part 8:   **Middle America**

Deep in the Heart of Texas   197

Summer School   211

Health Class   218

The Future   226

Afterword: Science, Religion and Race   235

Part One

L. A. County

Indian Wrestling

My first real job as a teacher was in a large inner-city school in the Los Angeles metropolis. It was 1960. Until then, the students I had taught were well behaved if not enthusiastic. As a practice teacher I had been assigned very limited objectives. I was expected to motivate the teenagers forced to put up with a teacher in training only temporarily—if at all. In the background there was always the real teacher. The students had to answer to this person if they gave me any serious trouble. Only when I got a real job did the full meaning of what a school really was and who students really were start to sink in.

This process began as a sudden clarity. It overwhelmed me during the first five minutes with my first class. There were thirty students, each fourteen or fifteen years old. All were quiet, but tension bounced off the walls. It was a scary but wonderful kind of tension. I had no idea what caused it, but I recognized it from when I was their age. For an instant I felt I was one of them, staring at me. I also knew that the tension had nothing to do with me. I felt excited and panicky at the same time.

The moment of clarity faded, but left me with the knowledge that I had been dangerously naive. I suddenly felt burdened by a responsibility for which no one had prepared me. I was caged with a powerful, wild, alien creature, which for some unknown reason lay dormant at the moment, but was totally unpredictable. I was alone with it.

Between classes, in the teachers' restroom, I sat in a stall and counseled out loud with myself. My second-period class seemed less scary. I knew I had a lot to learn but felt confident I could handle it. I was right on both counts. Had I realized how little I would ever be in control of my own fate in this profession, however, I might have resigned on the spot and gone to work for a large multinational corporation that was still recruiting me.

The first thing I had no conception of was that every school is actually two entirely separate institutions, located in the same set of buildings. One is the place where teachers and administrators work, and the other is the place where students live half their lives. The two groups' priorities aren't the same. This is why my fellow teachers were advising me not to smile during the first several weeks, nor to joke with students, nor to give them any freedom in the classroom. Of course I ignored their advice and smiled from the beginning. I also joked with students. I gave them lots of freedom, confident that deep down they shared my commitment to use our time together productively. I prided myself on treating students with respect.

No one had explained to me that the reason students seem well behaved at the beginning of the school year has nothing to do with their respect for authority. It has to do with their working out their own pecking orders. Although they may be acquainted with one another, in classes they aren't necessarily grouped with their friends. It takes awhile to form classroom liaisons and define leadership. My students had merely been keeping low profiles, getting the lay of the land.

Toward the end of the second week, misbehavior became rampant. I described the problem to my first-period class and asked them to join me in finding a solution. They looked blankly at me. A serious, small boy sitting in the middle of the class said, "Most teachers swat."

This meant hitting students on the rear end with a heavy paddle. I told them I had problems with this solution. It tended to prepare people for a prison environment, not the real world. "I have too much respect for you to swat you."

The class was silent. I felt inspired. I was brimming with love for them and they sensed it. My classes would set a new precedent at this school. Another boy, also with a serious expression, raised his hand. "Maybe you just don't have enough guts," he suggested.

During the next little while, I learned that students at this school ranked teachers according to how hard they could hit. Before the day ended, I discovered that every teacher except me knew this. They all swatted students as hard as they could, not to vent anger, but to receive a good ranking. Students behaved better for teachers who could hit harder-not out of fear but out of respect. It was a reward to the teacher from the students.

Next day I pointed out to my first-period class that they were all thirteen and fourteen years old. I on the other hand was in my twenties, not at all small, and in pretty good shape. "Do I have to prove to you that I'm stronger than you to get you to behave?" I asked them. Everyone nodded.

I sat on the corner of my desk and thought about it. They waited, like fans waiting for the bell to ring at

a prizefight. Finally I said, "OK. I'll Indian-wrestle anybody in the school. I'll give five dollars to anyone who
can beat me. If nobody beats me, will this prove I'm
stronger? Will you behave in my class?"

They stared at me, incredulous. Finally someone
said, "Yeah," and everyone agreed.

A girl on the last row pointed to the boy sitting in
the left front- corner seat and said, "Does that include
him?"

"Yes," I said, not hesitating. Although this boy
was taller and bulkier than me, he had a big soft belly
and a cherubic face. He was still only fourteen years
old. I have long arms and quadruple E feet. I have
always been a good Indian wrestler.

"When?" someone asked. "Whenever you like," I said.
"After school today behind the gym?" I said, "Sure."

That afternoon I showed up behind the gym,
carrying my briefcase. Within a few minutes I was a
white raft afloat upon a sea of black thirteen, fourteen,
and fifteen year olds. It seemed as though the whole
student body had turned out for this unscheduled
event. One short boy looked up at me and asked,
"Aren't you scared to be out here all alone with us?"

I said, "No," meaning it; but part of my brain
told me I was dangerously nuts.

Another kid said, "He must know karate."

I saw the boy I was supposed to Indian-wrestle
peek around the corner of the gym. Our eyes met. Then
he disappeared. The crowd and I waited for about fifteen minutes, but he never returned. Finally someone
said, "He's not gonna show up."

Someone asked if my offer still stood. I nodded.

"For how long?" They waited.

"A week," I said, feeling sick to my stomach. Then
we all went home.

The classrooms all opened onto a courtyard. Many students bought lunch from an outside concession stand. I was assigned to this stand for lunch duty. All week, between classes and at lunch, I accepted challenges to Indian-wrestle. No one offered any serious challenge. My classes started behaving as well for me as for the hardest swatters. I felt pretty good and pretty smart again.

Thursday, I volunteered for permanent outside lunch duty. Interacting with students was what teaching was all about. I ate a tuna fish sandwich every day, only because it was the best thing on the menu. By Friday I was nicknamed Mr. Tuna. On Monday of the following week, no one challenged me to Indian-wrestle. On Tuesday, while I was eating my tuna fish sandwich, a man I didn't know approached me. He said that he had heard about me and wanted to shake my hand.

I was struck by his appearance. My height, the color of gourmet coffee, he was built like a brick shit house. He seemed young to be a substitute teacher. I thought he might be a visitor—someone's big brother, maybe. It seemed strange he would be allowed the run of the school. This was a very strict school. In all the classrooms but mine you could always hear the teacher if he or she whispered. There was almost no teacher-student discussion, much less student-student talking. Wildness was not allowed between periods or at lunch. The playground was always filthy after lunch, however. The authorities couldn't solve this problem.

He took my hand gently and then started crushing it, one bone at a time. I willed myself not to react. I could not have outsqueezed him had I tried. He stared into my eyes. I hoped they showed that I was too professional and too disdainful to compete with him. Suddenly he released me. Grinning broadly, he gave me a friendly clap on the back, with tremendous pressure. My 4E feet saved me from lurching. I tried to look cool. Inwardly I started to panic. I realized that this man was a student.

The teacher on duty with me saw what was happening. He raised his eyebrows asking if I wanted to be rescued. I shook my head. I was aware that the black teachers at this school found me naive but entertaining. They knew I still didn't really have a clue about the universe I had entered when I came to work at this school.

My colleague nodded and sauntered off and my new "friend," having failed to break my hand or knock me down, signaled with his head to four or five more men I had never seen at the school. They came over and joined us. They were all built like him. He was their leader. Each of them in turn crushed my hand, and then they all accompanied me on my playground rounds, letting everyone know that I was under their protection.

That night, I composed a letter of resignation and called my parents. My mother heard me out and said that maybe I wasn't as compromised as I thought. "These kids are older than the other students because they probably failed repeatedly—or perhaps they dropped out and came back. But they're still kids. You can handle them."

I checked. She was right about why they were at the school. Later, I heard that there was even a student in his twenties, but I never met him. I realized that she was also right about these students being still inexperienced. They weren't certain of their physical superiority over me. None, even now, felt confident, I sensed, to challenge me at Indian wrestling. That's why I had had to Indian wrestle so many smaller students. These guys had sent them. What they were doing now was flanking me, reestablishing their authority by patronizing me. Two days later I got even.

My "friend" was hanging with his group when I walked up. He had just thrown a sandwich wrapper on the ground.

I said, "Hey man, why don't you pick that up?"

He looked at me as if I had just announced that I thought I had superhuman powers. Then his eyes became really cold.

"Hey, I wasn't serious," I said before he could react.

He looked at me, then at his buddies. His smile returned.

"I know there's no way you could pick that wrapper up. If you did, all these other kids would think you're soft. They'd be challenging you constantly. The truth is—you can't be sure you could handle it."

His buddies were all looking at him.

"You could lose your authority," I hammered the nail in.

My "friend" stared at me. He tried to look amused, but failed. His buddies watched like statues. He picked up the piece of paper and deliberately carried it to the garbage can. Then he picked up another. His buddies joined him. They cleaned the entire playground while everyone else watched in silence. Runners were sent to the lunchroom, and more students came to observe. No one made the slightest remark, even in a whisper.

Beginning the next day, for three weeks, my "friend" and his buddies supervised all the other students at cleaning the playground during my lunch duty. He explained to me that they did this to make me look good. "Even though you're stupid, you do have some class," he told me.

It turned out that the black teachers knew something else that I would painfully discover: This school would never hire me as a regular teacher. The only reason I was employed was because the school district had an arrangement with the university project I was enrolled in.

This project was a special teacher-certification program that recruited teachers who already had bachelor's degrees. Mine was in chemistry. Recruits took classes during the summer we enrolled followed by on-the-job training during the regular school year. This meant full time teaching jobs in the toughest school districts in and around Los Angeles, because these were the districts that cooperated with the program. They got discount teachers. The state paid most of my salary.

Two nights a week we attended classes. These were not ordinary education classes. All of us recruited at the same time always met in a seminar with only one instructor—our supervisor. What we discussed was not educational theory, but educational reality.

Regular teaching at the school I was assigned to was a pretty good job if one was black, but a low prestige job if one was white. All of the black teachers I met were good teachers and serious people. They did what they could within an insanely authoritarian structure created by the principal. One of the white teachers taught drunk; another lusted openly after his fourteen-year-old students. The principal was white. When I refused to swat students, he derided me openly.

Finally I wrote a letter to my supervisor requesting transfer to someplace that prepared students for life rather than prison. I showed it to the principal before mailing it. He begged me not to send it and said he would allow me to teach as I saw fit. Thoroughly frustrated by having to put up with my flaunting the written and unwritten rules that every other teacher in the school lived by, he asked me, face contorted with disgust: "Why do you want to teach these niggers, any-how?"

The Black teachers wondered the same thing, but from an entirely different point of view.

Motivations

A student named Lonald actually liked the subject I taught: math. Lonald was a skinny kid with an eager face. He always wore sneakers, blue jeans and a long sleeved white shirt with the sleeves rolled up. He learned everything I presented in class and craved more. He had a definite aptitude. He never flinched if I threw him problems he couldn't solve easily. Frustration only sharpened his enthusiasm. Outside of class we never communicated. Even so, I felt that we were like a good two- man band, we harmonized so well. Then one day Lonald's competence sharply nose-dived. He even began to misbehave in class.

I was confused and angry. I felt betrayed. For three days I secretly observed Lonald with his friends between classes and at lunch. I got a hunch about what the problem might be. I bounced it off the teacher on lunch duty with me, the same man who a few weeks earlier had respected me enough to allow me to commit suicide if that was what I wanted. He told me that my hunch was probably right. On the fourth day I cornered Lonald alone after class and told him that if he didn't straighten up, at least some-what, I would give him an A in math and also an A in citizenship on his report card.

"You wouldn't do that to me!" he half demanded, half pleaded.

For the next two six weeks I gave him Ds in math and Fs for citizenship, but his real grades were recorded in the office by the vice principal. Later I discovered other students who needed this grading flexibility. The problem was that Lonald needed to increase his popularity. He didn't want to be seen as a nerd. On the other hand, he didn't want to become one of the most truly respected members of the eighth grade either. These people never misbehaved in school. They were into really heavy things—illegal things, dangerous things—after school. They were too sophisticated to misbehave in school. Being a bad boy in school was safer if less prestigious. Lonald chose this route.

Another student who was bright but couldn't afford to have good grades on his report card sat at the back of my sixth-period class. Like Lonald, he was thin and sharp featured. Unlike Lonald, this student never made any effort in class. He also never misbehaved. He sat next to a girl he liked, but their socializing was circumspect. He showed no interest in my best presentations. He responded "I don't know" the rare times I called on him. His face looked more experienced than the other students' in the class. He was more self-possessed. He also projected an aura of intelligence that intrigued and challenged me. I thought of him as the quiet guy.

I asked other teachers about this student. They said I was right. He had a lot of ability. He was also one of the most delinquent students in the school, and smart enough to have avoided being seriously busted so far. Everyone knew he was into heavy activities.

I started calling on him regularly. Each time he shrugged and gave his usual response. He looked amused. One day I commented on his apparent interest in the girl next to him. He acted even more amused, but with some intensity. During the next week I called on him oftener and oftener, and made more comments. He kept his cool but stopped looking amused.

Thursday afternoon, after most students and teachers had left the school, I was still planning lessons. I looked up to find the quiet guy standing at my desk. We locked eyeballs for a few seconds. He wanted me to sense how serious he was. He said, "Man, I don't cause you any trouble in class. Why are you bugging me?"

I told him I could bug him if I wanted to, that I had the power. I said it amused me to bug him. I said that I was going to continue to bug him—that I would be like a big bug on his back for the rest of the year. He gave me a long cold stare and left. I knew that he was fifteen or sixteen years old, but I couldn't help noticing how he carried himself like a man.

The next day he cut my class. He came in late in the afternoon again. Without hesitating, he told me, very quietly, that the only thing he wanted from us honkies was the chance to kill us, to steal from us, to hurt us in any way possible. He was standing very close to me. His hand was in his pocket. I answered quickly.

I said that if that was indeed his goal, he could realize it more effectively with an education. Moreover, he had a right to an education. As a public servant, I was obliged to provide him with knowledge and skills to do with as he chose. It was not an imposition on him but a commodity he could demand. I advised him that if he decided to become a terrorist, for example, he would benefit by knowing some math. The leader of a terrorist group must take responsibility for handling supplies, logistics, all kinds of things that require math. People wouldn't respect him if he didn't know these things. And so forth and so on. It was a sales pitch. Slowly, his expression changed. For the first time, he looked genuinely amused. He took his hand out of his pocket, sat down, and thought about it. Then he told me how it would be. He would come in afternoons, late, and I would teach him. I would not tell anyone what we were doing, and I would continue to give him Fs on his report card.

And so it was. He came several times a week, learned quickly, and retained everything. He was brilliant and disciplined. I didn't quite honor our agreement, however. I handled his grades the same way I handled Lonald's.

Lonald was fifteen going on sixteen, and the quiet guy was nearly sixteen going on thirty-five. Both viewed education as a means to their ends. Another fifteen-year-old, somewhere in life age between Lonald and the quiet guy, completely rejected this view.

About the time Lonald and I worked out our compromise, while I was still harassing the quiet guy, this student shifted from trivial to serious misbehavior. He was not a leader. He wasn't a follower either, nor was he a clown, although he did clownish things. He was short, curly headed, and had a totally infectious smile. He performed for the class, taking their attention away from me. He was self-assured even when they gave him a weak response. At other times he engaged me in debate about mathematics.

"How come sometimes you use X̲s and sometimes you use dots and sometimes you use parentheses?" he asked.

"They are simply different ways to show multiplication," I answered.

"Who decided that? How come you don't use commas?" "Commas have other uses."

"How come?"

I gave a short presentation on the use of symbols in mathematics, how they are arrived at, and the fact that some things become conventions through usage. I tried to return to the lesson.

"Who was the first person who used X for multiply?" "I have no idea."

"How come? You're the teacher aren't you?"

"There's a lot I don't know. I'll try to find out and get back to you." Again I placed the pointer against the chalkboard beneath the problem and began my presentation again.

"OK. I see when you use parentheses and not Xs. How come you don't use brackets, like on page 86?"

"Convention." "Who decided?" "I don't know."

"So you'll find out?"

"I'll try." Back to the chalkboard.

"What about dots and Xs. How come sometimes dots and sometimes Xs?"

"If you blurt out again without raising your hand, I'll send you to the vice principal." I got through the presentation while his hand waved furiously. I ignored it and called on a girl in the third row to recap what I had said.

"I have my hand up like you said," he preempted her. "I don't want to call on you."

"You said you'd call on me if I raise my hand."

"No I didn't. I said that you have to raise your hand in order to speak. That doesn't mean I have to call on you."

"That's not fair. Do you guys think that's fair?" He turned to the class. No one responded.

"See, they don't think its fair either," he stated. I sent him out. Though he tormented me in class, he was friendly outside of class. One day, at lunch, I asked him why he tried to make it impossible for me to teach the class. He shrugged and ran off to chase a kid a bunch of other kids were chasing. That afternoon he came by after school late, like the quiet guy. He explained that he didn't entirely enjoy giving me a hard time. He spoke frankly and fluently, like a person who read a lot at a higher level than his courses required.

"As a person, you're all right. You really want us to learn something. You treat people with respect. But it doesn't matter what you do. You won't change anything. Public education is phony. I can't afford to have these kids start believing in it. You won't stay here anyhow. They won't let you."

I was impressed and made no effort to hide it. This teenager was a sophisticated political activist. "In other words, you want to force me to run my classroom like a prison, the way most classes in this school are run. You want to force me to be a jailer rather than a teacher."

He said, "You got it." He would have succeeded if I hadn't been able to get him transferred to another class.

The Solar System

Though the principal hated me, my university coordinator strongly supported me. The principal couldn't afford to alienate the university, so I was treated with kid gloves. Uniquely among teachers in this school, I was able to get rid of a student like the activist who competed with me for control of a class. The misbehavers that remained presented plenty of problems, but at least they were not determined to undermine my efforts to teach them.

In first-period class—regular math—four or five students would not stay on task, no matter how interesting I tried to make a lesson. Finally I presented the situation to the class and asked for suggestions.

"Its very difficult for me to teach the class when some people are having side conversations, putting on makeup, writing letters, drawing pictures, or passing notes to their friends. How can we solve this problem?"

"Send them out," one of the on-taskers suggested.

"I can't always be sending people out. The administration doesn't like it. They'll tell me to find another way to teach the class."

"Like how?" one of the off-taskers asked.

"I could give you lots of individual book work. You could memorize the terms in the chapter, and how to do the basic problems. Lots of memorization."

"We like the way you do it now," another off-tasker stated.

"But you don't participate," I said. "You distract everybody. Then no one learns anything."

"Just ignore them," an on-tasker suggested. "I'm getting a lot out of the way you teach."

"I like the way you teach too," another on-tasker affirmed. "I learn a lot this way."

What I was doing, basically, was a lot of group work, creative problem solving, dynamic applications involving the entire class in discussion, demonstrations, and projects. In short, lots of student-teacher and student-student interaction.

"I like the way we've been doing things too," I agreed, "but this method only works if everyone is focused and on task."

"I get lost," one of the off-taskers admitted.

"You can stop and ask me to go over something at any time," I said.

"It gets boring," she added.

"That's the real problem," I stated. "How do we deal with its being boring."

"You could make it more interesting."

"I don't know how. I spend many hours trying to figure out how to make it as interesting as possible. This is the best I can do."

"I like art," another off-tasker offered. "Why do I have to take math anyway? Why can't I just do art?"

"Me too," another off-tasker agreed. "Just send us to art this period."

As I was about to end the discussion and finally say something stern and authoritarian, the germ of an idea occurred to me. "Let me think about it," I said, and continued the lesson as best I could. The next morning, I made the off-taskers a proposal.

"How would you like to make a scale model of the solar system? We could draw it on the back wall."

"What's a scale model?"

"Its a model of something real made smaller or larger. Our classroom, for example. What if we wanted to draw everything on a piece of paper, to scale. Lets say you decided to make yourself five inches high instead of five feet high. How long would your pencil be?"

"About an inch," someone suggested.

"A lot less than that," someone else stated. "You'd have to measure," came a third opinion.

"Exactly," I confirmed. "Same thing with the solar system. You'd have to find out how big the sun really is and how big the earth really is, and then figure out how big the earth would have to be if the sun was, say, the size of a beach ball. You could get help with the measurement part, but you all would be in charge of the project."

"When would we work on it?"

"During class, while the rest of us are doing the regular work." "Cool!"

"Could we do it in color?" "Absolutely!" I declared.

"Wait a minute," a bright on-tasker raised her hand. "If you make it to scale, isn't Pluto gonna be on the other side of the school?"

"Actually, if the sun is the size of a beach ball, Pluto would be way downtown," I said, "but you get two bonus points for that inference." She beamed. They all knew what an inference was and that inferences earned bonus points.

"No, we'll just do it to size scale and not worry about distance. It has to fit on the back wall," I decided.

"So we can do it?" the obvious leader of the artists asked. "Do you want to?"

"Yeah, we'll try it" he said casually.

"Yeah," the other four nodded.

I didn't expect much payoff from this assignment. Mainly I wanted to involve the group at something productive, nonfrustrating, and doable. However, they took the project more seriously than I could have imagined. They were the first to class every day, and worked quietly and diligently the entire period. They didn't ask anyone to help them with measurements, and when they brought me their figures, the planetary sizes were way off. Then several amazing things happened: first, they wouldn't let me assign an ontasker to help them with the figures; second, they paid close attention when I told them how to approach the math tasks but would not allow me to actually solve the problems with them; and third, eventually they got everything right.

One morning they came in before school with a request. "Mr. Weiner, could you get us some butcher paper?" "Why do you need butcher paper," I asked.

"We're ready to start drawing for real," I was told.

I knew they had sketches on poster board and assumed they would transpose these to the walls, eventually.

The leader, a small handsome boy, read my mind. No way they're gonna let us paint on the walls," he said.

"Are you sure about that?" I asked. This possibility hadn't occurred to me.

"Check with the office," they said. "You'll see."

They were right. I brought them a roll of butcher paper.

They continued to work every day in class while the rest of the students did the ordinary curriculum. The vice principal, who had come up through the ranks of black teachers and continued to do dynamic things subversively when he could, dropped by occasionally. Sometimes he would chuckle and nod as he observed the class. One day he told me how much the principal hated having a group of students working independently in a class, most of the time sprawled on the floor.

Finally the mural was completed. It covered the back and side walls of the classroom. In addition to being accurate, it was exquisitely beautiful. In response to a call from the vice principal, the district office sent someone to take a picture of it. Ironically, the one who may have benefited the very most from the solar system project was the principal.

Parents

In algebra, students were struggling with word problems. I changed the seating arrangement so that four desks were grouped together. Each pair of students, not each group of four, worked at the same level. I posted answers on the board and told the students to figure out how to arrive at these answers. I was merely applying what I was learning at the university: that often people think better when they can verbalize.

The method worked. When students asked for help, they would say, "Don't tell us, just give us a hint." Mostly they asked those sitting in front or behind them for hints. You could never hear anyone whisper in my classes. You had to talk loudly to be heard. The principal called my university supervisor to come and control me. My supervisor loved what I was doing. The principal instructed the classes near mine to close their doors.

In direct contradiction of the productive atmosphere and the real learning going on, test scores were always terrible. Finally I asked third period, my most mature class, what was going on.

"I know you understand the material!" I communicated my feeling of frustration. How dare they deny me evidence of their excellence—and mine!

"Test anxiety?" a girl in the back row timidly suggested.

"No way! There's no way test anxiety explains the difference between how well you do in class every day and your pathetic performance on tests!"

There was always deep quiet when I innocently raised a question involving fundamental characteristics of the system. Finally, a slightly plumpish girl with a beautiful round face and eyes filled with feeling, named Melanie, spelled it out for me: "Our parents are used to us making bad grades. We start making good grades all of a sudden, they'll get all excited. They'll start expecting it. We like this class—its different. But you won't stay here. Then we'll hate math again, and make bad grades. We don't need to be getting our parents all worked up when its not gonna last."

Her position was not political, just pragmatic. She was the second student who knew with certainty that I would not stay at the school. I knew she meant that this would have nothing to do with my wishes. I asked if everybody in the class agreed with her diagnosis of the situation. They all nodded. I told my other algebra classes about this discussion. They said that Melanie's answer was correct.

Sunflower Seeds

One day in first-period class I grabbed a handful of sunflower seeds from a student. I told her—and everyone—that there was a school rule against eating in class. They blatantly ignored it. Since I knew how much they respected school rules, I assumed there must be something special about those seeds they were always eating. I wanted to share this wonderful experience. I popped the whole handful in my mouth.

Everyone stared at me wide-eyed. Chewing, I stared back, pleased. I continued to shatter stereotypes, continued to show that a teacher can be a human being, continued to challenge the sick tradition of authoritarianism they were accustomed to at this school. For once, you might have been able to hear the softest of whispers in my class, except that I made a lot of noise crunching up the seeds.

Finally they were crushed enough so that I could swallow. It took a while to get them down. When I could speak, I said, "I can't imagine why you eat these things. They have no flavor and a terrible texture!"

No one said a word. They just sat open-mouthed. I started to wonder if I had been too radical. Finally, a student who was usually shy, raised her hand.

"You're supposed . . ." she began quietly. Then she couldn't hold it back any longer. ". . . to take off the shells first!" she finished in a shriek.

They were all howling. They fell out of their seats and into the aisles

All day—in fact, all week—I received grinning, giggling advice about how to eat sunflower seeds from students and colleagues. One teacher offered to tutor me in the art. The only people who didn't make a big deal of it were the students in my third-period class. They hardly mentioned it.

James Meredith

Third-period algebra class was different from fifth or sixth periods. Third-period students seemed more grown-up, but they were also a little less motivated. The other classes slightly outperformed them. It always took a while to settle sixth and seventh periods down in order to start the day's lesson. Never third period. They came in quietly and did their work quietly. Sometimes I didn't have to raise my voice at all to be heard in that class. They were too quiet.

Efforts to loosen them up failed. If I told a joke, they listened politely. Students never thought my jokes were funny, but in other classes they expressed disgust. No one in third period called me Mr. Tuna. Then, one day, things changed.

Third period came in noisily. I had to request their attention three or four times. Finally they were quiet, but the atmosphere was intense. First- and second-period classes had behaved as usual, but third period was definitely different. I asked them what was going on.

"James Meredith," was the terse explanation I received.

29

The governor of Mississippi's refusal to obey a court order allowing James Meredith to attend the state university had not even flooded the media yet, but it turned out that third period not only knew what was going on, they were vitally interested. "You are discussing these events in your history or social studies classes," I assumed.

I assumed wrong. They told me that they had not and would not be discussing any of this at school in any class. A student said he had heard that some teachers might be meeting with interested students away from the school.

I asked them if they would like to talk about it now. They enthusiastically would.

Mostly, their discussion that day was a sharing of information. "My cousin's down there."

"My brother says he's goin' down there tomorrow."

"My dad says no good is gonna come of it. He won't let my sister go."

"My mom wants the whole family to go, but Daddy says we can't afford it."

"I think he's crazy to go to a white university."

"Why crazy? That's where you get the best education?"

"Uh uhhh! You can get just as good an education at Howard or Tuscogee."

"Yeah, but you pay more. He's a Mississippi citizen. He's got a right to go there."

"Why go where you're not wanted?"

"Why not? He's got a right to an education. Doesn't matter whether they want him or not."

"Yeah, but its hard to be somewhere you're not wanted." "That's why he's a hero."

They debated and argued heatedly but with self control. Each wanted to hear the others, as well as to be heard. When the bell rang, I asked them if they would like to continue this discussion tomorrow.

"Yes! Yes!" the whole class shouted.

They ran out of gas about ten minutes into the next period. Someone turned to me and asked, "How could the governor do that? It's against the law."

I said that the answer to this question would take some time. It would have to begin with some history, which might not seem immediately to the point. I knew they preferred short answers, that they didn't like to be lectured. Unfortunately, I couldn't deal with this question briefly. Would that be OK?

They agreed, though a few were skeptical.

My presentation was academic and undramatic, far less entertaining than algebra presentations. But now I felt them completely. I outlined the history of African Americans beginning with slavery, stressing the economic correlates of discrimination. They hung on every word. Their eyes gripped me. Every pore was open. I didn't talk down to them. A student would interrupt if she or he didn't see a connection or wanted me to repeat something.

I moved fast. The next day I told them that I wanted them, based on the information they'd received so far, to try to answer the question: What are the fundamental reasons why people like James Meredith, and themselves, have to fight for the rights that others receive automatically? I would help but not direct them. When someone stated a hypothesis or an argument, I would help ensure that the next person to speak addressed this argument and did not change the subject. When they got stuck, I would encourage them to reach within themselves and drag forth ideas intuitively. I would tell them when one of their thoughts indicated a promising direction. Then they could explore it until the reason I thought so was clear, or they could state why they disagreed with me.

We proceeded this way for three full periods. The original question was finally answered satisfactorily if not comprehensively—at about a college sophomore level. I told them that they had done a good job and that I was prepared to have more class discussions. "I see a reasonable connection between algebra and discussions," I stated. "Algebra is logic. Not just a unique way to solve only one kind of real-life problem. Part of the reason you learn algebra is to be able to think more effectively. In this way, algebra is useful to everyone. Even to someone who knows for certain that they won't ever have to solve a single algebra problem for the rest of their life once they leave school. You could call algebra a form of pure logic. A properly conducted discussion is also an application of pure logic. Therefore there is no inconsistency between a good discussion and algebra."

I didn't know how well this rationale would stand up to curricular scrutiny, but if discussion of social issues motivated this class I was determined to try it. "There is one condition," I told them. "We have to get all the algebra done. If we finish algebra by Thursday, we'll have discussion on Friday."

I told the vice principal about third period. He applauded my curricular innovation. He also told me that without my umbilical attachment to the university, I could never get away with it..

Third period had many discussions that year. They also became my top performing algebra class.

Melanie

Next Friday, third period hit the ground running. Someone wanted to discuss sex. The same Melanie who informed me that students were obligated to protect their parents from the trauma of temporary good grades wasn't sure this was a good idea.

"He's trying to be fair with us. Don't take advantage of him."

Several students nodded. Voices said, "Yeah, right." No one argued. I thanked Melanie and told them they could discuss any topic "so long as your purpose is to understand it better. This includes social and cultural behavior, psychology, physics, chemistry, astronomy, anything. Our purpose is analysis and logic. Nothing is taboo."

They were mainly interested in the connection between sex and love. It turned out that even the boys were pretty love and relationship oriented. I gathered they had seen a lot of sex without much love. Although they touched on every aspect of sexual behavior, there was no giggling or showing off. They were curious to know how one another felt and what one another believed. These were things they didn't casually discuss among themselves. They asked me questions about venereal disease, but nothing personal.

In the future, in school districts where people hailed from higher strata of society, students the same age giggled a lot. They asked if I had affairs, if I lusted after female students, if I ever had a homosexual experience. I answered most questions in some fashion, but especially the underlying ones: "Is it normal for men old enough to be my father to want me sexually?" "Do all married men have affairs?" "Might I be gay?"

"Is being gay terrible?" Third-period students didn't have these concerns. At other schools later on, some students asked frank questions to expose me as a poser, a closet tightass. They expected me to be shocked and angry. Often they were shocked when I answered their questions in detail: "How long is the average penis?" "Why won't girls do it when they're on the rag?" "Why do dogs eat turds?" Sometimes a student observed that this kind of question was immature, and I would point out that immaturity is a natural state for fourteen and fifteen year olds, and nothing to be ashamed of.

This observation did not apply to third period. They were way beyond these kinds of questions. They were the most mature teenagers I ever taught. Sometimes I wondered, in retrospect, if these students had experienced too much of life, too early. This conclusion did not jibe, however, with the fact that they were much less cynical than their better-heeled counterparts of my acquaintance in the future.

Third-period students, and the students at this school in general, seemed at ease with themselves and with one another. They had fun at school dances. They treated one another with affection. They didn't worry much about who liked whom. They weren't afraid of hard truths. The majority of students I taught later on, of all ages, found it difficult to discuss serious issues. They preferred not to know what a discussion might reveal. More than once, someone asked, "How can you stand to analyze all this stuff all the time? Do you really want to know these things? Doesn't it make you depressed?"

Third-period class didn't find it necessary to wear rose-colored glasses in order to feel good about life. They never complained about having too much knowledge. One day Melanie brought us back to the discussion about James Meredith. She said, "I've been thinking about it. Isn't it possible that maybe we really are inferior? I mean, why do we always get the dirty end of the stick? I don't think I'm inferior, but maybe I am."

Many teenagers hate themselves. Not Melanie. She was unusually self-possessed for someone her age, neither humble nor brash, and definitely not self-effacing. Her question was simply logical. If we were being truly and honestly analytical, it had to be asked. The answer could change her life. She would not be able to accept it dispassionately. Her face was serious and calm. I imagined that Joan of Arc might have resembled Melanie. The class was sober. Melanie was in charge. They would not jump ship as it entered these dangerous waters.

We began with a hard look at slavery. How it worked. Why the slaves didn't fight back. The class learned how American slave owners had systematically separated captives from the same tribe. The slavers also separated family members. They violently rooted out seeds of tribalism whenever they appeared. Slave owners kept their captives demoralized.

"How come they treated them so bad, if they thought they were just basically beasts?" a student asked. We had already talked about the slaver rationale: that enslavement actually improved the lot of Africans, who were little better than beasts, and that slaves could never develop much, although exposure to white society improved their character somewhat. "Seems like they were afraid the slaves might get together and fight. How could they organize and fight if they were as dumb as they were supposed to be?"

Everyone agreed that this was an excellent point. Slave owners must not really have believed their slaves were inferior beings. They said they did, but they behaved in an opposite manner. They used the kinds of tactics and strategies that one must use to control people who are courageous and smart, and are only at a disadvantage so long as they lack weapons and are few in number.

"But once they were free, why didn't they make more progress?" a girl on the first row asked.

The boy sitting next to her shared what he had learned from his history teacher, though not in history class. "This book," holding up his history text book, "is full of . . ." He looked at me. ". . . baloney. It says the Civil War was fought to free the slaves. They just used that as an excuse. It was all about economic control. The freed slaves had nothin'. Nobody tried to help them. Everybody used them some way or another. Lincoln didn't care anything about black people."

I expanded upon his points and added details.

"I never really realized some people can totally control other people, and they can't do anything." A girl observed.

"My father's way too hard on his parents," her friend noted. "He's always tellin' em they were a bunch of Toms."

"Bull! You can always fight," a boy who looked angry said.

They debated this question. Next Friday, someone brought in a book about other peoples who had been persecuted throughout history. The class concluded that, as tragic as it was, people could be truly helpless—at least for a while.

"Still, black people were the slaves, not white people," a tall boy pointed out.

I gave a presentation on genetics. There wasn't much to debate. Everyone agreed that there did not seem to be any biological basis for the idea that skin color indicated that people had different competencies or drives. A student found documentation that whites had been slaves of blacks from time to time.

"Why would anybody want to make somebody else a slave in the first place?" asked a girl on the second row, who had said nothing until now.

I reminded them that this was the fundamental puzzle we were trying to solve.

"Fear," someone stated. "People are afraid of anybody different." "Are you?" I asked.

"Maybe. It depends."

"Would you want to make a slave out of someone different that you were afraid of?"

"No! I'd just want them to stay away from me."

"How many people does anybody here know personally, that would make somebody a slave because they were scared of them?"

No one could think of anyone who would do this.

"Power," someone suggested. "People want power over other people. The strong always conquer the weak."

"Do you want power over someone?" I asked. "I'm not in that position," he answered.

"Lets say you were on a desert island with a kid littler than you. Would you make him your slave?"

"No. I don't want a slave!"

"How many people in here would like to have a slave?" One boy started to raise his hand, but changed his mind.

"Do you think that this class is an unusual sample of human beings," I asked.

Everyone agreed that it was not.

"Actually, you probably are," I said, "We'll talk about how later. How many people in here know someone who would like to have a slave as a power trip?"

This time a few hands went up. Collectively they knew about five people that fit this profile.

"So it stands to reason that very few people would enslave people just to have power. There must be another reason."

No one could think of any.

Finally a boy in the back of the class said, "They made money off the slaves."

"So you think people would enslave other people if it was profitable?"

Most of the class thought so. "How many of you would do so." No one raised his or her hand.

"How many know people who would do so?"

Most of the students raised a hand. Collectively, the class estimated that they knew at least a hundred people who might enslave other people for profit.

For the next two Fridays, I helped them to develop this insight. They discovered that not only slavery but present-day racial discrimination had been— and still was—economically profitable. They learned that many social institutions as well as individuals participate in maintaining this profitability. They also learned how their class was different than a group randomly selected from the population as a whole: they 100 percent rejected the appropriateness of discrimination for profit.

Melanie asked, "Why didn't our parents ever tell us about this stuff?"

"They were ashamed," the girl beside her stated. "They thought maybe they deserved to be treated that way."

I asked Melanie if her original question was answered. Did she think that black people's experience could be the result of some essential inferiority on their part?

"Doesn't seem likely," she concluded, like a good logician.

Then she asked me, "Do you really like teaching us? Wouldn't you rather be someplace where the students are like you?"

The girl next to her gasped.

"She has a right to ask that question," I said. "It's logical. Maybe I'm just trying to make things look good so you'll like me. Maybe I've loaded the dice so they'll come out right. She's right to be skeptical. If I really care about you, I won't do such a thing."

"So what's the answer?" a boy on the first row pressed me.

"You tell me. Your own intuitions are your guide. Trust them. No one can really fool anyone. Deep down you know better than I do how I feel about you."

No one said anything. I waited. Someone smiled, someone stretched.

"You like us," Melanie said. The bell rang.

The Vice Principal

One afternoon, the vice principal invited me to go for coffee. About ten years my senior, in his middle thirties, he was a very dark skinned, powerfully built man a little shorter than me. We went to a drugstore and sat in a booth. He ordered coffee and pie à la mode, and I had a soda. He began to talk about himself. He described the shit he had had to eat year after year as a minor administrator always on the verge of dismissal. He talked philosophically about how education should be done. He told me how intensely he had always wanted to change things.

He told me that some teachers in our school were doing great things with groups of students privately — teaching them about their background, about their possibilities in a real way, without pretense, hype, false promises. He told me I had contributed to this effort. I had given my students something valuable. I had described some of the backstage machinations of those who control things. "You are in a better position than your students — or me, for that matter — to observe these things," he said. "Your being who you are is useful."

I said I regretted that I would not be hired by this school or this school district. I would not be allowed to make any sort of contribution. I lacked his strength: he had the know-how of teachers who learned how to teach subversively because they had to.

"You can develop these skills," he advised me, "if you want to badly enough." He wasn't certain I should worry about it all that much. "You're lucky to have options. Don't dismiss them casually."

I said I guessed he was right about my having a bird's-eye view of racism. I told him about being brought up a Jewish boy in a southwestern city. From an early age I knew I was different from most white people. However, I was often treated as an insider. From the age of twelve I worked at all kinds of jobs. I was always included automatically when bosses or coworkers or customers told disparaging jokes about black or brown people, or raged over paying social welfare to support them, or grieved about being the true victims of people with money and power.

My best friends in high school shared my liberal attitudes but weren't Jewish. They got into heated arguments when people told racist jokes around them. No one ever argued with me. They became silent. On more than one occasion I was told that it was well known that Jews were nigger lovers. Finally, I realized that when I was with my friends I was like a guest at a family squabble. Although I was treated like an insider when it came to sharing racism, I wasn't treated like an insider if I argued about it. By the time I came to Melanie's school I had been present when white people from all religious and social class backgrounds rationalized racism.

The vice principal said that the principal defined the student body en masse as potential revolutionaries, anarchists, rioters, savages. He tried to imagine and eliminate every possible opportunity for the expression of latent or covert violence. Every incident of overt violence vindicated his resolve. My classes alone were interactive, dynamic, and noisy.

The vice principal liked my university supervisor. He mentioned that my supervisor had been to observe me quite often. The vice principal suspected that my supervisor was sending glowing reports to the principal, with copies to the district superintendent.

I said maybe that explained a pattern I had noticed. Almost invariably, a few days after an observation by my supervisor the principal would call me in and remind me that I was uniquely pampered in his school. Alone among all the teachers in the school, I did not have to deal with troublemakers in my classes. For me, the dilettante, they were removed.

The vice principal chuckled. "And the illogicality of his position never occurs to him. If troublemakers were removed from everybody's classes, all classes could be interactive—the way they should be." The vice principal said that forcing teachers to keep disruptive students in classes was a widely used technique for controlling discussion. The principal considered it absolutely outrageous to be deprived of it. I think that in the vice principal's eyes this was my major contribution to the school, though he gave my supervisor more credit than he gave me. He wished universities could have more impact upon school policies than they did. This was our last conversation. The school year ended a week later. That summer I finished my course work at the university and obtained a teaching certificate. My next job was very different.

Part Two

The Bay Area

Hillary

My second paid professional teaching job was in the wealthy suburbs south of San Francisco. The school, though a public school, was tastefully built and breathtakingly surrounded. The students arrived in Cadillacs and Ferraris. Hillary reminded me of Melanie. Thinner, and more delicately built, she had charisma, charm, beauty. She wasn't as serious as Melanie or as knowledgeable about life. But she was open, had a good sense of humor, and cared about people in the same way. Melanie was quietly happy. Hillary was bubbly. She was a year younger than Melanie, and her family was definitely upper caste. Like most of the families in this school, they were white, Protestant, and wealthy.

Melanie's parents were supportive, loving, intelligent people. So was Hillary's mom. I met her at back-to-school night, along with nearly all of the parents of my students. At Melanie's school, they didn't have back-to-school night.

The parents at back-to-school night were articulate and well informed. A few, like Hillary's mom, wanted to know how I planned to teach regular math or to talk to me privately about their children. What a number of them were most interested in, however, was the "new math." They had another son or daughter in the school in honors math, where this avant garde approach was being used. The parents could not understand, much less solve, these kids' homework problems. Since the parents could easily afford tutors, their help wasn't essential. Apparently they simply wanted to be informed. I gave a short presentation. At the end of the evening, a small group returned and asked if I would be willing to meet with them on occasional Saturdays. I suggested that it might be more appropriate to ask the teacher of the honors class. They said they preferred me. I agreed happily. I was honored and flattered.

I should have been nervous. Early the next week, the principal summoned me. He had received a call from the district math coordinator. I smiled. Actually I glowed. Already in my new job I was about to be commended. The principal said that some parents had asked the coordinator if they could compensate me for teaching new math to them a couple of Saturdays a month. The principal was smiling too. Then, still smiling, he informed me that the coordinator was not happy about this. In fact, he was seriously pissed. He had made it clear to the principal that any such program would be initiated by him, not by some brand new teacher. I stopped glowing.

The principal asked me why I thought the parents had approached me. I supposed because the honors teacher didn't want to do it. He continued to smile at me, not even slightly fooled, and said nothing. He knew I thought the parents were dazzled by my presentation. I hastened to describe how I had urged them to try the honors teacher first. He said he appreciated my willingness to take initiatives and realized that I was new to the district and still naive about procedure. It might be best, in future, if I would run initiatives by him. He was no longer smiling, but he had a twinkle in his eye. He wasn't really concerned about this incident. He didn't mind seeing the math coordinator caught with his pants down. I was free to return to my duties.

Although he had lit a cigar and started doing paperwork, I didn't leave immediately. I asked why he thought the parents had approached me. He looked up and regarded me not unkindly but tiredly, the way the vice principal at Melanie's school had when I first sought his counsel. He wasn't certain I was worth the effort. "What you have to understand is that some of these honors students act smug as hell." He returned to his work. Our interview was over. He expected me to figure out the rest for myself. This took a while, it turned out. The politics of this school were like, but also different from, the politics of Melanie's school.

If Hillary reminded me of Melanie, the principal reminded me more and more of the vice principal at Melanie's school. In order to survive, he had to honor other people's priorities. He had to cover his ass at all times. In this school district, priorities were defined in terms of position and status. He didn't care about status; he cared about education and about students. Upper-level administration cared intensely about status. The parents who wanted to learn about the new math cared less about their children than about not looking dumb. I was a safer resource than the honor's teacher. The honors kids wouldn't be able to pump me as easily about how their parents were doing.

In many of my new students' homes, there wasn't much interaction between children and parents. Parents gave their children spacious bedrooms, huge lawns, basketball and tennis courts, swimming pools, sumptuously equipped playrooms, lots of pocket money, and just about anything else material they wanted. But children interacted mostly with governesses and other servants. Students in Melanie's school had practically no pocket money and they lived in tiny, poorly insulated houses. They interacted with their parents a lot—sometimes too much. But when relations soured, they had aunts and uncles, cousins, grandparents, and neighbors to turn to. If these were not the same as parents, they were not servants.

Hillary's classmates were aware of being rich. They talked a lot about the things they got. They had acute knowledge of who was who in the class—whose parents didn't have money and whose profession, like mine, had low status. They talked about the parties they had at each other's houses on weekends. At fourteen, they'd apparently had more sexual experience than I'd had at twenty-seven. They also drank a lot. I checked around and came to the conclusion that some of this talk was nonsense. Some kids were into heavy stuff—drugs and sex—but many were posing. They posed about other things too, it turned out.

Science class was usually bored and withdrawn. One day they behaved like third period had in Melanie's school, the day James Meredith became famous. They wouldn't settle down. Several students came in discussing something intensely, and others gathered around to listen and interject. It was a personal issue in this case, not a social one. They were sharing experiences of harsh punishments received at the hands of their parents. They outdid each other describing pain and suffering.

Finally, I imposed order. I said we could devote the period to their discussion, but the entire class must be brought up to date. The boy at the center of everyone's attention described how last night, out of boredom, he and a friend had started throwing lit matches at one another. They eventually set his bedroom on fire. The fire department came immediately, but the mess was horrendous. His parents were called home from a party. He couldn't lie his way out of it because his little sister saw them do it and eagerly told on them.

Students hearing the story for the first time reacted exactly the way those who had already heard it reacted when it was told to them. Everyone wanted to know only one thing: "What did they do to you?" Their faces lit up with anticipation and expectation. It was the first time I had ever seem them excited.

Laughing was rare at this school. Even school dances were tame affairs. At Melanie's school, dances created a carnival atmosphere. Students had huge fun together. Hillary's classmates acted cool and sophisticated. Even when describing wild parties, exotic sexual encounters, and unrestrained use of controlled substances, they weren't nearly as excited as now. The boy retold the story, adding elements of punishment he hadn't included the first time. In particular, how he was locked in a dark closet for more than eight hours. I was horrified. His parents were sadists. His classmates looked gratified, some even wistful. Then another boy told a story about how he had been terribly punished several months ago. A girl followed him. Everyone was enthralled. They were happy. They were having fun. I was incredulous.

"Wait a minute," I finally shouted. "This is nonsense. I don't believe it. I know your parents. They don't punish you that way. In fact, they rarely punish you at all. Why are you saying these things?"

Silence. Something fundamental was about to be imparted to me. An expensively dressed girl pointed to another girl in the class. She said, "Her parents do." The girl she referred to was not part of the in-group. She was considered a nerd. Everyone knew she had limited television-watching privileges, was not allowed to go to wild parties, and had a curfew. She often complained about these cruelties. Suddenly she was the star of the class. They demanded to know, in detail, about her life under discipline. She didn't know how to respond. She thought they wanted to make fun of her some more. Then the expensively dressed girl said she had always been jealous of the girl with strict parents. Her own parents didn't care what she did. "I could burn down the house. They'd just buy another one."

Other expensively dressed students nodded in agreement. The girl with supervising parents admitted that sometimes she was glad her parents cared enough to punish her when she did something really bad. She didn't like all of their strictness, however. She told the class about her suffering for thirty minutes. They consumed her words. Just before the bell rang, the boy who had burned his bedroom admitted that his parents had not been all that upset. He hadn't even been grounded. Several students said that their parents never yelled at them, but sometimes their maids did.

Hillary missed several days, including the day the punishment discussion took place. In this school, classes were taught by wings. Everyone in my wing had me for science and math; therefore I thought she might have heard about the discussion. Because of her reaction to something I told her, however, I realized she hadn't.

For several weeks before her absence, Hillary was a different girl. She was morose rather than cheerful, bad-tempered rather than reasonable, defiant, argumentative, bitchy. She wouldn't talk to me. I had already learned at Melanie's school that teenage girls go through mood swings regarding their male teachers. One week they adore you which is wonderful, even though you know not to take it seriously. The next week they hate you which is even more difficult to ignore. As a student, I had adopted the modern view that the Oedipus complex is an interesting notion but hardly a scientific theory. As a teacher on the front lines, I now completely accepted its validity. However, as it turned out, this was not what was affecting Hillary.

I ran into Hillary's mom at a party for a retiring teacher. She asked how Hillary was doing in class. I told her. She said Hillary was a hundred times worse at home. I asked if there had been a major change in their lives. There had. Hillary's mom had remarried. The decision had not been sudden, and she had thoroughly included Hillary in every way. Hillary had adored her new father when he was a fiancé, but as soon as they began life as a family she became impossible. Hillary's father was bending over backward to make her feel secure. Hillary's mom felt the situation had deteriorated into one of pure appeasement. Hillary was pulling strings like a puppet master. Her mom was about fed up.

Hillary's absence occurred shortly after this conversation. When she returned to class, she was her old self. After a few days, I mentioned to her that she seemed happier than she had for a while. She said this was true, looking radiant. Without thinking, I said, "I bet you're getting punished more lately." Her eyes became huge. "How did you know?" she asked.

One afternoon after classes, a beautiful young woman walked into my classroom. She was dressed very elegantly. She was stopping by on the way to an appointment to discuss her son, who was failing. As I got out my grade book and began to bring her up to date, she stopped me. She said, "It's OK—I believe you, I know he's failing. I wanted to tell you I have complete faith in you. Please make him do what he's supposed to do. Do whatever you think is necessary. You have my permission to punish him. In fact, I would appreciate it if you would."

I told her that the school and parents have to work together. Punishing her son was her job. She stared at me for a moment, wondering how to get through. Her look conveyed frustration, pain, even anguish. She said, "But he gets so angry with me!"

The Petition

I did several things that one of the teachers on my wing wasn't happy about. The first was to stay after school tutoring students. I had time and it was no big deal, but my colleague felt I should know that this practice was not endearing me to everyone. For my own good, I needed to be aware that some teachers— not my helpful colleague, of course—felt that I was making them look bad. They were as dedicated as anyone, but being married with children didn't leave them much spare time. My staying made it appear they were less dedicated than I. The second thing my colleague was concerned about resulted in a summons from the principal. I wasn't making students line up when they left my class as I was supposed to. I admitted this sin and promised to try harder. I didn't even remember until the next period. A few days later I saw the principal standing in my wing, watching my students go chaotically by. He never said anything more about it.

A friend told me my colleague had speculated in the faculty lounge that the reason I played basketball with students in the gym during lunch break was to suck up to them. In Melanie's school, no one had noticed where I ate lunch. The idea that I had always eaten outside in order to suck up to students would not have occurred to anyone. At Hillary's school, I went to the basketball court for exercise. As a result, I got to know the basketball coach and we became good friends. In addition, I did successfully suck up to one student.

I had not played much basketball as a teenager. I was built for football and had been a good tackle. I didn't know much about basketball. My most troublesome student, who was failing both math and science, was a star basketball player. At first he was surprised to see me on the court at lunch, then disdainful. When he realized I was serious, he began to teach me. He was patient and considerate and quit hassling me in class.

The way he had hassled me was by instructing other students to do things surreptitiously, like put a tack in my chair or throw something when my back was turned, or take something from my desk and never return it. I knew he was responsible and he didn't try to hide it. He was never rude, always cool, even when I got in his face on one occasion. As I became a better basketball player, he stopped being subversive and his grades went up.

One reason for this was because he stopped worrying about looking bad. Maybe my unconcern about looking bad on the basketball court impressed him a little. He was a good athlete, but had never been a good academic student. He let people know that he could be if he wanted to be, but that academics weren't his priority. He was one of those people who have to excel at whatever they do. Better not to try than to try and fail. I could tell that in science class he was often interested in spite of himself. He admitted this one day on the basketball court. I asked why he thought that might be. He said it was because of my teaching approach: "You don't make us memorize stuff all the time."

This was true. My approach, in both math and science classes, was to maximize discovery and minimize rote learning. I told him that there were different teaching techniques and different learning styles, and maybe I had hit upon his. Maybe the reason he was less bored was because this was the way he liked to learn. If so, he could probably make good grades in my class. He was skeptical. What if I was the only teacher who taught this way? I told him that educational philosophy was moving in the direction of emphasizing reasoning skills. In college, especially, students who could think well would have an advantage. Students who made A's in high school only by memorizing often didn't succeed in college. It was the thinkers who did better in college. On the other hand, not everyone needed to go to college. I asked him what he wanted to be someday. He said an engineer.

Like the quiet guy in Melanie's school, once sold he excelled. He made B's the next six weeks, and after that A's. He was embarrassed at first. I told him about the students in Melanie's school who had two report cards, one public and one secret. He understood completely.

I was not always so successful. One day after school, three young ladies paid me a visit. They approached me in a formal manner, and one of them carried an official-looking piece of paper in her hand. They were all the same five feet two inches tall, dressed in expensive but modest dresses, and trim and athletic; and they all had turned-up noses and shining faces that would have been almost identically pretty if they hadn't been wearing such severe expressions. Their document was a petition. All had signed it. These girls were straight A students except in my class. They had especially high status in the class of my concerned colleague down the hall, the one who liked students to line up.

Their petition was simple. They would appreciate it if I would teach math properly, the way their former math teacher had done. I asked what this meant exactly. They fidgeted some and then explained to me, almost in one voice, that what bothered them especially was being shown various ways to work math problems, and then being given choices on tests. They wanted to be shown the correct way, be allowed to memorize it, and then repeat it on a test. They thought it improper, moreover, to be asked to make up their own math problems, especially test questions.

I tried the same pitch that sold my student who taught me to play basketball. They looked at me blankly. I began again. I told them that they were all obviously intelligent people; otherwise they couldn't have done as well as they had in school. Like many people who were good at doing things a certain way, they felt a little insecure about trying something new. They didn't need to worry. If they would give the new way a chance, I was certain they would soon get the hang of it. They didn't buy this idea for a second.

Finally I told them that this was the way the class would be taught all year. I hoped they would decide to adapt. They informed me that good students in the school considered me to be strange and also probably incompetent. I should take advice from other teachers. They marched out of my classroom, turned right, and disappeared into a classroom down the hall.

They never gave in. They consistently made B's in my class, and bore them like crosses. The colleague who had given me advice began to look at me with an expression close to fury. Toward the end of the semester, the principal called me in again.

The complaint he had received this time he could not brush off. Status was too heavily involved. Three of the school's worst students— and worst behavior problems—were making straight A's in math classes taught by me. Their aptitude/IQ tests were low and their emotional stability questionable. Their families were comfortable but not wealthy. The school counselor had already suggested that they might be happier elsewhere. Apparently a deliberate campaign had been aiming toward this solution when I entered the scene. My helpful colleague, who no longer made an effort to be civil, was its spearhead.

The principal informed me that he had no problem with the way I taught and did not take kindly to the pressure being brought to bear on him. However, unless I could validate these students' grades, he would have to pay a heavy price in order to support me. He had greater leeway than the vice principal at Melanie's school, the principal also had more enemies. They would have loved to see him hung on his leeway. Like the vice principal, he knew the difference between being effective and being a martyr. I showed him test papers and described in detail how the tests were administered. We went over them for more than two hours. He told me to continue what I was doing. There was no twinkle in his eye.

About a week later, the parents of one of the undesirables visited me. They had accepted the idea that their son had learning problems. Now they were perplexed. Suddenly he was excelling. I showed them the same evidence I had presented to the principal. Without thinking, I suggested that they might want to take him to a nearby university, one of the top-ranking ones in the country which had an excellent testing and guidance facility. I told them that its measurement of learning traits would be a good deal more precise than our school district's.

Two weeks later, the principal summoned me again. He asked if I had advised parents to go to the university's testing and guidance center. I contritely admitted it. He glared at me. He was serious and angry. He told me never to do such a thing again without his permission. Then his face softened. All three sets of parents had taken their sons to the center. One son turned out to be a bona fide genius; the other two were exceptionally bright. He said the math coordinator was furious and scared shitless. The principal invited me for supper that night and later fixed me up with his niece (which turned out to be a bad idea). He would have hired me for the next year, had I not decided to go back to school for a higher degree. I think he missed me but didn't entirely regret my decision.

The Meensom Boys

The reason I decided to go to graduate school was that an old friend of our family came to give a lecture at a nearby university—the same university that had tested the students my school district defined as dumb and deviant and found them to be smart and valuable. He was the dean of one of the ranking schools of social work in the country. I told him about my experiences so far in education, and he told me that I needed to get a graduate degree in sociology. "That's your field, the way you tend to look at things. Call me when you've got it. I'll have a job for you."

What he said was true. I had looked at things sociologically since the age of four. We were friends with a family named Meensom in those days. My dad and I went dove-hunting with Mr. Meensom. One time, driving back, a six-foot diamondback rattlesnake stretched across the road. Mr. Meensom shot it and gave me the rattles. Another time he shot his dog with rock salt for not retrieving fast enough.

The Meensom boys were nine and ten. We had great climbing trees in our yard. They would take me with them high in the trees and tell me that the only way I could get down was to jump. I knew better than to jump, which disappointed them. I couldn't get over the fact that even though they were nice to me and seemed genuinely to like me, this didn't take precedence over their savage curiosity. Seeing me fall to my death—possibly disfigured, bloody, in pain, etc.—was more interesting than anything about me alive. I assumed then and there that this kind of orientation was one of the things that differentiated some people from others. To be safe with people like the Meensom boys, you had to be one of them. I knew that I was different: I would not enjoy seeing another person hurt or killed, whoever they were. I wondered what made us different.

Years later, I was a scoutmaster for two years. My troop was from the wrong side of the tracks. We were sponsored by one of the city's business clubs. Many of my scouts had never been more than six blocks from where they lived, seen the lake in our town, or been fishing. Their world was more violent than the one I grew up in.

One day, a boy named Jorge came to the meeting singing a song that simply repeated the same phrase over and over to a ridiculous tune: "Sapo, Sapo, sácame, Sapo!" Eventually it became irritating. I asked if there wasn't more to the song than "Frog, Frog, get me out, Frog!" Jorge explained that it wasn't really a song. He had just made it up. Earlier that day, he was playing in the street when a paddy wagon drove by with a young guy from the neighborhood in the back. He was clawing at the wire on the open back of the van, yelling to his friend on the sidewalk, Sapo, to come bail him out. The guy's yelling had stuck in Jorge's mind.

With one exception, the scouts in my troop were not violent people. There was one boy, however, who was bigger and older. Most of the time he helped the younger kids, and I treated him pretty much as my assistant. Occasionally, however, he did hurtful things, or caused hurtful things to happen, to one of the others for his amusement. Like holding someone's head under water to see how he would react. The kids kept a wary eye on him, and were pretty good at staying out of his way when he got bored.

Except Henry. Henry didn't accept the nature of things. He felt it was unfair that he should have to suffer periodically just because someone was bigger. He was always crying, always complaining. I interceded. I appealed to my assistant's sense of decency and fair play. I threatened to lower his status, even to expel him from the troop. It wasn't working.

Finally I told Henry that what he had to do was get really mad. He had to get so mad that his adrenaline flowed. He must become attacker rather than victim.

Henry glared in disbelief. You're crazy!" he declared. "He'd kill me!"

"No I'm not crazy," I retorted. I explained that a bully isn't angry when he bullies—there is no adrenaline flowing. When adrenaline flows, even a weak person becomes strong. I told him that I had witnessed this phenomenon with my own eyes.

"One night, these five macho guys in my fraternity." "What's a fraternity?" Henry interrupted.

I explained what a college fraternity was. "Anyhow, these guys were all jocks. They sneaked into the room of this brother they considered a nerd. He'd just gotten engaged to this really beautiful girl that one of the machos liked. But she never ever gave him even a glance. Anyhow, they were going to throw him in the lake."

"They were gonna drown him?" Henry was wide-eyed.

"No, no," I explained. "It was a tradition to throw people who got engaged in the lake. Only not this early in the year. See, the lake froze in the winter, and the ice had only melted about a week before. The water was freezing, even though it was warm outside. Anyway, the nerd woke up when they grabbed him and he totally panicked. He started hitting, biting, scratching, and ripping those machos. He grabbed a chair and ripped it apart and beat the crap out of them with it. Before his adrenaline ran out, he put four of them in the hospital. The other one ran away."

I had Henry's full attention. "Now here's my point," I concluded. "Ordinarily that guy couldn't have fought his way out of a wet paper bag. But when the adrenaline flowed, he was a superman." Henry appeared to think the story was interesting but irrelevant.

A couple of weeks later we went on a camping trip. I was supervising the unloading of supplies from the bus when I heard someone yelling for help. The voice faded, getting farther and farther away. I scanned the area. On the far side of a large field, just entering the woods, my assistant was running as fast as he was able with his hands held up around his head. Henry was smaller and faster. He had a large branch in his hand, and was whacking my assistant every chance he got.

During the following weeks, my assistant complained about Henry's relentless aggressiveness. So did the other kids who had picked on him. He fought them all, rarely winning but hitting so hard that everyone knew it would be very costly ever to bully him again. He was a changed man. Henry and I had both learned that sometimes the only way to deal with people like the Meensom boys is with adrenaline.

The officials that maintained the atmosphere at Melanie's school were not unlike the Meensom boys. They did not consider their students to be people like themselves. They were unresponsive to the kind of reason that drove my life. Had I somehow been chosen to join their elite ranks, I could not, for any salary or reward, have conformed to their policies. I wondered how people became committed to carrying out such policies.

At Hillary's school education had a higher priority, and in classrooms it was done a good deal better. But not better than it was done informally, after hours, by teachers at Melanie's school. In Hillary's school, students' unhappiness was not a great concern—status was more important. If you weren't a member of the in-group, it didn't matter whether you succeeded or failed. I could not have been a member of the powers that be that defined things in Hillary's school district either.

The vice principal at Melanie's school would not have survived as a member of his district's top level staff. It was one thing to keep a low profile and do what was possible between the cracks in the system, and another to help set and reinforce bad policy. The principal at Hillary's school was no different. He could not have survived as a member of his district's administrative elite. He could not do what was expedient if it conflicted with his values. Why were these people's values so different from those of their superiors? Why didn't they place self-interest ahead of idealism, as they were expected to?

I realized that my friend the dean was right. The way things were was not going to change through persuasion. The vice principal at Melanie's school and the principal at Hillary's school had accepted this fact and were willing to do what they could. I still operated with a lot of adrenaline. I wasn't ready to accept their realities. Unlike Henry, however, this would only get me swatted like a fly unless I changed my theater of operations.

Part Three

Graduate School

Sociology

I applied to several graduate schools but wound up at my hometown university in Central Texas, where I had already shown the ability to obtain an undergraduate degree in chemistry. The building housing the sociology department was just as old as the chemistry building but a lot less odorous. All of the teaching and research assistants had offices on the east end of the third floor or on the fourth floor. The more senior students had offices on the fourth floor, and that was where the most interesting discussions took place. This was where we really learned what sociology was all about. One of the first things I learned was that modern sociology had no place for questions that could not be asked scientifically.

Karl was the most fanatically scientific graduate student in our department. He applauded sociology's repudiation of all that reeked of intuition and sub-jectivity. He kept the books on his desk and shelves precisely arranged, along with everything else in his office. His blond hair was always perfectly cropped. Gene, whose long black hair was always as messy as his office, regularly sneaked in and made subtle changes to Karl's order. He found it as ridiculous as

Karl's academic ideology, which might be appropriate for physics but was not for sociology. If sociology could not deal with issues of value and nuance, it was a worthless exercise—not really scientific at all, merely scientistic. Robert, whose brown hair was medium length and neat but not nerdy, could see both sides of the issue. He predicted that while Gene's view had merit, Karl's would prevail. He was right.

Gene wasn't opposed to science; he simply felt that its definition had to be broad enough to include ideas that could not be scaled in a way that would satisfy a physicist. For example, social status. Anyone could tell you that the chairman of the board of Du Pont had higher social status than one of Du Pont's factory workers. What no one knew is exactly how many degrees of social status each possessed. "There's no such thing as a unit of social status. It can't be defined quantitatively. Does that mean it doesn't fucking exist?"

Karl said that if social status was defined as years of education or as dollars of income, it could be scaled. "An income of $50,000 could indicate twice as much status as an income of $25,000 dollars per year. Twelve years of education could mean twice as much social status as six years of education."

Gene pissed on this argument: "You know damned well twice as much income doesn't necessarily mean twice as much social status! I'd rather not study it at all than stick phony numbers on it just so it'll fit into a mathematical model."

"My point exactly," Karl replied calmly, unflustered by Gene's vehemence and well aware that his smugness infuriated Gene. "It would be better to abandon softheaded concepts altogether, but if you insist on using them, you have to scale them." He said that if sociologists wished to achieve respectability as scientists, they had no choice but to scale all of their variables, even if this meant sterilizing certain concepts, in some people's opinion.

Gene said that Karl preferred scientifically precise nonsense to knowledge that made sense.

Robert agreed with Karl that it might be preferable if social status was quantified, but that if it could not be quantified, this should not keep sociologists from studying it. "Hell, society runs on status."

"On the other hand," Robert continued, "even if the damn journals are full of precise nonsense now, maybe their goals aren't wrong. Maybe someday we will have precise knowledge."

Red headed Cassandra, who was a year ahead of the rest of us and considered these debates sophomoric, said boredly, "Right. In about a thousand years. Meanwhile, shall we just assume that all social planning has to be totally capricious? Or shall we just stop trying to deal with everyday human problems until they can be quantified?"

Whatever our personal views, it was clear that our professors wanted us to learn scientific methodology. If we wished to self-destruct in the fruitless search for other ways to deal with sociological questions, we could do that on our own time after graduation. The journals would not publish—and the foundations would not fund—many studies of a qualitative nature. Privately, some professors wondered whether sociology was being stripped of dead wood or simply sterilized of meaningful content by the present trends. They did not, however, foresee the possibility of even a limited resurgence of the rich scholarly methodologies of the past. They advised their students to go with the flow. "Don't be obstructionists." My questions about the Meensom boys, about the powers that be, about happiness would not find a home in modern sociology.

I asked Robert why he thought important questions were ignored in sociology simply because no one could assign numbers to them. Robert said that it was because we live in an age of science, and science rules. "Science has become a religion. People believe it in, whether it makes sense or not."

Bill and Cynthia, the only married couple in our department, were reading C. Wright Mills and had a different perspective. They felt it was all political. They reminded us that the first people to deal with social issues were philosophers. One of their main concerns was ethics. Shortly after the Renaissance, some radical philosophers began to criticize the way nation-state heads exercised power. The ruling class retaliated. Since the field of physical science was ascending like a rocket, the state created a new kind of science: social science. It certified social scientists as its official scholars. Henceforth these new scientists were the only ones qualified to think, write, and speak about social and political matters. Philosophers in particular were thereby defined as unqualified to do so. "Since the ruling class had total control of sociology's purse strings, they just made sure its objectivity favored state policy."

"In other words," Gene summarized, "the fat cats purposely invented sociology to put a stop to political dissent."

"Exactly," affirmed Bill and Cynthia. "Traditional sociology never did a decent job of probing into anything important."

Cassandra and Robert thought Bill and Cynthia went too far. Karl thought they were subjective and not to be taken seriously, although the fact that Cynthia was a superb statistician made him uncomfortable. He couldn't resolve her skills with her point of view. The fact that both Bill and Cynthia looked like sandy haired Greek gods didn't help either. Gene agreed with Bill and Cynthia completely but was afraid that nothing could be done about it.

Bill and Cynthia felt that the situation was not hopeless. We all needed to read Marx and Mills, to begin with. Sociology had produced whores for the state but also powerful dissenters. "Sociologists who fought the establishment paid a heavy price, but in the final analysis they did a better job than the old radical philosophers at critiquing power. Radical sociology is already too entrenched to be uprooted by the main stream's obscene love affair with mathematical modeling," they assured us.

These kinds of discussions rarely surfaced in seminars. In seminars we took turns writing papers to be offered up to our peers like tender sacrifices. We ravenously tore these morsels apart, under the pleased bloodshot eyes of our professors. Sometimes they allowed us to devour published articles, written by prominent sociologists. This was the most fun. We learned statistics, symbolic logic, and stochastic modeling. Among ourselves we engaged in dialectics. We debated everything our professors professed. We analyzed their articles and books and followed their rises and falls of status within the department and the profession. We learned quantitative methodology from them, but did qualitative analyses of them. Even Karl participated, drawing intuitive conclusions right along with the rest of us.

Years later, a physicist told me that sociology was not a real discipline. It was not a science and not an art form. I said that for me it was a way to try to be systematic about things that can't necessarily be dealt with scientifically. He said that this statement had no meaning. The term "systematic" meant scientific, which meant quantitative. I thought of Cassandra, and asked the physicist if he agreed that the vast majority of planning decisions that people make every day, individually and en masse, cannot now or in the foreseeable future be predicated upon quantitative analysis of any kind. He agreed that this was probably so. "Are these, then," I asked, "necessarily merely capricious decisions that we make? Is human progress forever doomed to be accidental? Or do you think we operate mainly on instinct? Or are we guided in all matters by a supernatural being?" He said he would not subscribe to any of these causes. "In that case," I said, "you had better hope that the idea of being systematic, without necessarily being scientific as you narrowly mean it, is not absurd." He had no answer. It was the only time I ever won an argument with a physicist.

No one strove harder to be both scientifically rigorous and down-to-earth relevant than Professor George. His body of work, which was impressive, reflected a genuine desire to understand society, not just to reduce it to quantitative variables. He was built like a tank, and was tough as nails with his students, but I suspected that he had a soft heart. On the last night of his course, he threw a party for us at the home of one of the students. About eleven o'clock,

Thad challenged him to an arm-wrestling match. Professor George said that he didn't arm-wrestle unless there was money involved. Thad had been a truck driver, among other things. They bet five dollars. Thad lost. About one o'clock, Thad was teetering on the curb, puking up scotch. Professor George appeared in the doorway. He had a look of real concern on his face. He came over to Thad and put his arm around him. He said, "Thad, don't forget that you owe me five dollars."

Love

One day Robert walked into my office, which was next to his on the end of the third floor, and told me that he had just analyzed some data which confirmed something he had suspected. Apparently, one of the elevators was in love with him. Since Robert was brilliant but also crazy, I wasn't completely astonished at this statement. But it did pique my curiosity. I asked him the question he wanted me to ask: "How did you arrive at this conclusion?"

For several weeks Robert had noticed that the elevator was usually waiting for him when he went to call it. He hypothesized that while unusual, this was nevertheless a random phenomenon. In sociology, this is called a null hypothesis. Even though you hope something is happening, you hypothesize that it isn't. If your null hypothesis doesn't hold up, you're in business. Robert began to collect data. Statistical analysis showed that the chance likelihood of the elevator being ready for him as often as it had been was less than one in a thousand.

In studies published in the major sociology journals, the failure of a null hypothesis at the .05 level of significance (chance occurrence less than five times in a hundred) is generally taken to mean that something may be happening. Null hypothesis failure at the .01 level of significance (chance occurrence less than one time in a hundred) means that one's career is definitely not jeopardized by concluding that something is probably happening. Robert's null hypothesis had failed at the .001 level of significance! I suggested that someone was probably observing him leaving his office and sending the elevator to him. He said he'd neutralized that possibility. He had the computer generate a schedule for using the elevator and the stairs in a random fashion. He followed the schedule religiously. When he randomly chose the elevator, it was waiting.

Claude, who wore his coal-black hair in duck-tails and spoke with a country twang asked how Robert could be sure it was he the elevator loved. Maybe it loved all of us. Robert said he'd also checked that out. He was certain that he was the only one especially favored by the elevator. Claude and I both observed that he hadn't asked us any questions about our elevator use. Had he asked other graduate students? Robert said that he had not trusted anyone except himself to collect reliable data on this phenomenon. He himself had observed all of the graduate students with offices on the third and fourth floors using the elevator. He did this on random occasions, according to another schedule spit out by the computer. He found that the rest of us had to wait an average of half a minute for the elevator.

This did seem fairly conclusive, since our building only had four floors. We told him it all looked pretty tight. He ought to publish. He said he was thinking about it. We were never sure he wasn't serious.

Claude had the office next to Robert's. He was the only teaching assistant who was already married. He was about our age, but already had several children. He was a devoted husband and father and a person of great decency and integrity. He was more interested in healing society than in studying it scientifically. This caused him some problems in the department, which didn't worry Claude at all.

We were always popping in on one another, but sometimes Claude was hard to catch. He had a stream of beautiful girls flowing in and out of his office all day long. Robert and I asked him about this early in the year, but he just said that they were students coming in for counseling. Gradually we got used to it, but fourth-floor graduate students who came down now and then were amazed. One day a particularly beautiful student emerged from Claude's office, buttoning her shirt. This time Robert and I couldn't restrain ourselves—we had to know what was going on.

Claude was grading papers when we converged on him. He looked calm enough but was sweating a little. He explained that the student had wanted a higher grade, which Claude couldn't grant. She had offered to earn the grade unconventionally. Claude had demurred. Finally she stood up and took off her shirt. She wasn't angry—just wanted Claude to know what he was missing.

Like the rest of us, Claude taught introductory sociology. What was different about his classes was that an unusually high percentage of his students were girls from small towns, like Claude himself. Apparently he was famous among them and they selected his class. It wasn't because he was an easy grader; they just felt comfortable with him. This was real sociology. The esoterica we discussed on the fourth floor paled by comparison with it.

Shula

During the summer of my second year of graduate school, my grandparents offered me a trip to Israel. I agreed to go because I could do an interesting master's thesis there. I set it all up ahead of time. My grandmother also thought I might meet someone special. I made it clear that she was wasting her money. At this point in my life I was in search of data, not romance.

In Haifa, my brother-in-law's best friend, Kenny, showed me the sights. He said that when I went to Tel Aviv, I had to request one date with his fiancé's cousin, Shula, or else he would be in trouble with the family. Behind his back, his fiancé's family called the cousin's family and implored her to go out with me because I was a family friend and a lost soul in Israel.

Shula had just returned from a year of working her way around half the world. She had embarked upon this adventure partly to escape the mounting pressure to get married that every Israeli girl experiences after puberty. She had tried to get across to her parents and relatives the fact that she had no intention of marrying just because already married women didn't see why she shouldn't be as miserable as they were. Maybe one day she would have a child, but she wasn't about to saddle herself with a husband just to satisfy convention. She told her family that if they fixed her up with any more blind dates she would leave again.

In short, without having spoken, much less met, we were agreed to dislike one another at first sight. To start things off on the right track, I didn't phone when I was supposed to. Shula had made it clear to Kenny that she would not waste a perfectly good weekend on me, and that I had better call well in advance. She'd work me in on a weeknight. When I didn't call, she decided that Kenny had idiotically told me that she would be available over the weekend. Out of a sense of decency and respect for Kenny's prospective in-laws, whom she loved dearly, she waited around. Actually, he had told me nothing except to get in touch. When I finally did call, the following Tuesday, the first words she ever uttered to me, after "Hello," were "Where were you?"

The effect of this was a vague feeling of chaos sweeping over me. It wasn't unpleasant. I felt that I was supposed to know how to answer her but didn't. It didn't matter. She didn't really want to talk, just to get our date arranged, accomplished and finished. Without preamble she told me when to be at her house, where it was, and what bus to catch to get there. She said to tell the bus driver and he would let me off at the right place. She didn't ask if I agreed, only if I understood. I said I did and she hung up. Our date was for that very evening.

Shula, to this day, has no sense of quantity. She always misses amounts of things by magnitudes of anywhere from ten to a thousand. She miscalculates distances by inches or miles and time by seconds or hours. I had gathered from her instructions that her house was a ten-minute ride from my hotel. I told the driver the name of her street and got no response. I told him again and got no response. I told him a third time, and he said something in Hebrew that sounded impatient. He realized that I didn't understand and told me in English that he had heard me the first time. He would tell me when we got there. "Sit down and enjoy the ride." I sat down, feeling the chaos growing deeper.

Riding the bus was not boring. Tel Aviv is a busy, dirty, interesting city. A lot is always going on. All of a sudden I realized two things simultaneously. First, that we had been riding for much longer than ten minutes. Second, that many of the people on the bus were staring at me when they thought I wasn't looking. Some of them stared even when I looked straight at them.

The reason was because Shula's neighborhood— actually a kind of suburban enclave called a *shikun*— was not a ten-minute ride from the heart of Tel Aviv, but nearly an hour's ride. All of the people on the bus were from there. They knew Shula. They also knew about a hotshot from America who was coming to take her out. Shula had been the star of the shikun from the time she was little. These folks were not automatically optimistic about my value to her, much less about my intentions. But I had no clue about any of this at the time. It just added another dimension to the chaos.

Finally there were only two people left on the bus, an old woman and myself. I approached the driver again. Before I opened my mouth he said, "Sit down!" The city lights had long since faded. I was pretty sure I knew what was going on. I was going to be left alone out in the country to find my way back to the hotel. The bus driver didn't like American middle-class

Jewish boys who had never fought in a war or gone several days without water or been hungry or life-threatened in any way. I didn't blame him. But I did start thinking about which way I ought to walk when he finally dumped me, which was about a minute later.

The bus stopped, the doors opened, and he said, "Get off!" I was reluctant, so he shouted, "Hurry up!" I got off, the bus doors slammed, and he was gone. Laughing, I imagined. There was nothing around me but trees, and the street was full of sand, like a beach. I had no idea which way to start walking. Then I felt a hand tugging at my sleeve. The old woman had also gotten off. She spoke to me in Hebrew. Then some European language. I tried Spanish. Pay dirt! She was from Bulgaria. I explained my plight. She shoved me through some of the high bushes beside the road and told me to wait a second. I could see a building. People were sitting on porches. She spoke to one of them and returned to where I obediently stood. She took my hand and led me to some stairs, then up the stairs and to a doorway in a building. She said that this was the place. I asked if she was sure, the chaos was swirling and eddying around me. She gave me a concerned look and left.

I raised my fist to knock on the door. Before it could strike the surface, the door opened with a swish. A beautiful, perfect sized girl in white filled my vision. Hazel eyes took me in sternly and a lovely mouth, not smiling, said curtly, "Come in. I'll get my purse." In a flash she was gone, revealing the room behind her. In its very center, legs spread apart, hands on hips, stood a giant. The chaos surged, and took on tinges of panic. The giant glared at me. Then his voice boomed out in English with a Russian kind of accent: "I understand you're from Texas?" I nodded. "Then where's your horse? Ho! Ho! Ho! Ho!"

For an instant I had been absolutely certain that I was about to die. I had no idea why, but there it was. Then his big face opened wide and he laughed and the chaos disappeared. Shula's father's fingers were each as large as three of mine. Yet I never saw anyone lift a baby as delicately, or smile as sweetly at their grandchildren as he did in the very near future. How he intended to treat me on that occasion I never found out. Shula reemerged and swept me out of the house before I could shake the huge hand reaching out to me. I glimpsed a small, delicate woman behind him who was smiling and waving vigorously as we receded down the sidewalk.

Down the steps, onto the sandy street, into the bus, and back to Tel Aviv. Shula never stopped talking or let me get a word in edgewise. She did public relations work for an international vocational training institution which had a large, successful operation in Israel. Shula's job was to squire wealthy Americans and Europeans around its facilities. She knew how to focus people's attention where she wanted it. Now she focused mine on the sights and sounds of her shikun, which had about as much interest potential as a sandpile. She even found some way to comment on the black countryside between the shikun and Tel Aviv. Once in Tel Aviv it was easier, and I thought I could sense her relief.

She had no intention of totally wasting an evening, especially since I was paying. She took me to the kinds of places she enjoyed. We listened to wonderful music, ate incredible food, saw fantastic old buildings. She never allowed a pregnant silence to exist, only ceasing to make small talk when our attention was riveted upon one excellent entertainer or another. But she screwed up finally. She expressed an opinion, the first of the evening. It was an offhand comment concerning American culture. I said I didn't completely agree with her. It was a reflexive response. Had I thought about it, I probably wouldn't have said anything. She was on some kind of roll, and I was afraid of what might happen — to me as well as to her — if I messed with her.

She stared at me for a split second and then got back on track, pointing out a derrick on top of a building, indicating the inception of a new apartment complex. Fascinating stuff. And it was, actually — or rather, she was. I had never met anyone so aggressive and graceful, so enchanting and forbidding, all at the same time. After about fifteen minutes she asked, "What do you mean you disagree? How can you disagree?" I started to explain why I disagreed. After twenty words or so she cut me off with a shrug that said "You're obviously full of shit!" and turned to a more interesting topic — an old couple crossing a street that Ben Gurion had once lived on.

But she couldn't leave it alone. She loved arguing even more than she hated giving me the vaguest idea that I might get a foot in the door. Our first interchange set the tone for the whole of our relationship. It was a no bullshit debate. I was already in love with her. I was already afraid of her as well. This didn't mean, however, that I assumed she had any emotional or intellectual depth, or skill, other than a kind of insane creative ability to turn small talk into filibuster. Now she gave me a chance to know her. Soon I was impressed as well as infatuated. She had as much courage as Melanie, as much dignity as Hillary as much integrity as the vice principal, and was stunningly beautiful and fiercely intelligent. I realized I had no chance with her. But somehow, miraculously, I was wrong. By midnight we were sitting in a dingy little place on upper Ben Yehuda Street eating the worst spaghetti either of us had ever tasted, and not caring. We were talking quietly now, learning about each other.

I never made it to Hebrew University to do my thesis. We got married six weeks later. Since our engagement had been rather short, we discovered a few rough edges on our honeymoon. We fought and made up all across Europe. Fortunately our areas of fit were powerful and compelling. Otherwise we probably would have killed each other. By the time we got home, things had actually become fairly blissful. When I returned to graduate school, everyone cautioned me against planning any more studies abroad. Then we went to a graduate student party.

It started out well enough. Everyone liked Shula immediately. They thought she was beautiful, smart, loved her accent, and wanted to know if she could shoot an uzi. She lied and said she couldn't. She got whisked away by one group, and I joined a discussion in progress. After a while I noticed her standing with another group, a frozen half-smile on her face, and still later with another. I didn't think much about it.

About an hour after midnight, the party broke up. In the car, Shula was quiet. I assumed she was as tired as I was. The evening had been full of drinking and talking. It was summer and still hot. I commented on how warm summer evenings have a soporific effect.

She asked, "What does 'soporific' mean?" I explained that I meant the weather makes one sleepy. She exploded. "Why couldn't you say that, then? I never had problems with English in London, New York, Chicago, or anywhere. But you people speak some strange language that is totally beyond me. Everybody was talking about some theory of social conflict. What do you know about social conflict?"

She was right. We didn't speak English, we spoke sociology jargon, which is impossible and pretentious. So were our clinical discussions of social conflict. Shula's life had been filled with social conflict. Much of her family had been wiped out because of it. In Lithuania, they hadn't even waited for the Germans. They chased her father's village into their synagogue and set it on fire. When she was growing up, her father worked for the British police but passed information to the Israeli underground. Often she ran messages for him after curfew. When she got caught, he had to publicly spank her in order to allay suspicion. She had marched across the Sinai Desert and lived in a foxhole. Sociology graduate school was mostly a bunch of white, Anglo-Saxon, middle-class young people with no lines in their faces.

One of the graduate students, however, did have lines in his face. He was a Jesuit priest and spoke normal English. Shula enjoyed joining in our late-night conversations about theology and philosophy. When he and I enrolled in Professor Green's seminar, Shula agreed to help us out with our project. Professor Green was a big name in sociology. He had recently come to the department, and people were standing in line to study with him. The seminar project involved searching through student records in a local junior high school and high school. Our goal was to discover whether student labeling by teachers carries over and affects student success in school. Our group had the high school. It was tedious work. Shula agreed to carry on for us when we had to stop our search and go teach a class.

Both participating schools had only black students and faculty. Most of the files were in an office next door to the vice principal's office. All day long Shula would watch students troop in and out, receiving punishment swats, like those meted out to students in Melanie's school. They didn't seem to mind all that much, although sometimes she would hear a grunt or a squeal. Finally, she asked the vice principal how he justified hitting everyone all the time. He said it was necessary. She couldn't understand this. He smiled and shrugged. She continued to ask him. She wouldn't let him off the hook. Finally, he sat down patiently to explain the facts of life to her.

I could have told him this was a mistake. Shula sucked him right in. They had a long argument and became friends. They continued to have lengthy conversations and ate lunch together. She showed him pictures of her parents, sister, brother-in-law, their kids, and me. He showed her pictures of his mother in her coffin. When we finally finished our work at the school, they parted ceremoniously and agreed to stay in touch. None of the rest of us ever got to know anyone in either of the schools.

Professor Green gave a party at the end of his seminar. When I went over to introduce Shula, he already knew who she was. He told her that if she would formally register for his course, he would give her an A.

Intergroup Relations

One of my professors recommended me for a part-time job with the university's extension division. They had an adult basic education program whose major project was conducting training workshops for teachers of adult students. These students were usually black and had less than an eighth-grade education. The teachers, on the other hand, were mostly white. Ideology did not motivate most of them to seek the job. They were in it for the low salary. Many were as prejudiced as the principal of Melanie's school. Unlike the administrators that ran Melanie's school district, the state adult education commissioners were seriously concerned about this fact. Teachers' racism reduced student enrollment. States received federal money for adult education. Therefore student enrollment affected state budgets. The state directors asked the extension division to help them deal with this problem.

Most of the teachers who attended my workshop sessions were there through no choice of their own. They sat quietly with closed faces, not looking at me or at one another. Growing up, I had always been afraid of such faces. If you didn't show the right attitude they might never look at you again, or kill you. I began by introducing prejudice as a normal, often positive human attitude. Prejudice in favor of someone was often good, I pointed out. It amounted to giving people the benefit of the doubt. The participants began to think, "Maybe this particular asshole sociologist isn't all that liberal." I went on describing instances of good prejudice. One or two participants actually joined in and provided more examples.

Casually, I changed direction. I observed that prejudice against someone might not be so good. No one, after all, likes to be prejudged. I asked for examples of times when those present had been prejudged and hadn't liked it. There weren't any responses. Suspicion filled the room. They weren't stupid.

I persisted in speculating about good and bad prejudice. The reasons for good prejudice were obvious. What about the reasons for bad prejudice? Such as mothers-in-law against mates? Bosses against employees? Oldtimers against newcomers?

I stayed away from controversial topics. Some participants finally joined in. At one time or another, such nastiness had caused nearly all of them some pain. They were glad to have a chance to talk about it. They agreed that the reasons for negative prejudice were not hard to identify: rigidity, insecurity, stubbornness, as well as opportunism and meanness.

Then I asked, "What about race prejudice?" Stony silence. I said that maybe this was really a different kind of thing than the kinds of prejudice we had been talking about. One or two hopeful glances.

"Damned right, it's different!" the glances said. "It's just being honest about how God made the world." The little glimmers of hope faded, however, as I launched into a psychological analysis of racial prejudice, ignoring its economic dimensions for the moment. I asked them to recall how some people seem to need to have someone to hate. They all knew people like that. I explained that psychologists believe that racism allows people to express anger safely. Like kicking the dog. Or beating the wife. Or raking the employee over the coals. They all knew about this sort of thing, too. I said that people who discriminate often have deep-seated feelings of inferiority. This hit close to home. Tension mounted.

I twisted the knife. Only a few people, I informed them, are really so insecure that they have to hold onto racial prejudice. Many white Southerners still feel inferior as a group. This isn't the same thing as being an inferior individual. Even when white Southerners don't actually feel prejudiced, they think they have to continue to act prejudiced. They have to practice discrimination in order to show group solidarity. If they aren't better than blacks, they're nothing. Taut faces, tight lips, you could have cut the tension with a switchblade.

But things are changing. White Southerners don't have to make a show of force anymore. The new South is run by corporations, not carpetbaggers. Corporations hire people because they're smart and get the job done. Blacks pose no threat to whites. Unless, of course, whites are actually inferior to blacks and can't risk competition. Two participants walked out.

Nowadays the costs of being prejudiced outweigh the benefits, I concluded. Prejudice just tends to keep people in the Dark Ages. Therefore, with the exception of whites who probably really are inferior to other people, most are able to give up their prejudice. Two more walked out.

I knew the people I was talking to; I had grown up with them. They couldn't reject these arguments—some, secretly, did not want to. They knew it was all true. I wasn't going to convert anyone. My goal was to separate those who could be rational about racism from those who couldn't be. The extension division and the state directors didn't mind. It was a way to separate wheat from chaff.

Always my section of the workshops was one of the best-liked, as well as the one most hated. The national adult basic education convention that year invited me to give a presentation. This resulted in several invitations to conduct workshop sessions in states outside the domain of the university that employed me. One was from a southern state, and the workshop was held in the state's second-largest city. There were more black participants than usual.

We met in an elementary school in a poor section of town. The person in charge, a large black man with a sombre face was not from the State Director's office, but was someone local. He was equivalent to a principal. He treated his staff and students with dignity and respect. During my portion of the workshop he stood at the back of the room and scanned the audience. It wasn't clear from his facial expression what his thoughts were. Afterward, he said he thought it had gone well and I felt he meant it. But I also sensed that for some reason this didn't give him much pleasure. I thought the session had gone particularly well. Though three participants sat utterly mute and immobile, like ugly alabaster statues, throughout the whole analysis no one had walked out.

That night, late, the phone woke me in my hotel room. The voice simply said, "Leave town." When I arrived at the workshop the next morning, I reported the call. I assumed I should simply ignore it. The sombre faced man said, "No, you'd better take it seriously." I thought about it. I thought about Melanie and the students in third-period class. I decided to stay. The bad guys would not run me off. Then the vice principal's image popped into my mind. He was shaking his head gently from side to side. He had an amused, tolerant smile on his face. I left town before sundown.

The next morning the adult education team members were sitting around the long table in the extension division. I told them why I was back a day early. Before anyone else could say anything, a young woman who had recently joined the team turned and looked me in the eye. She said that she had worked for a project where she and two black men had traveled all around the South doing workshops. They drove together, ate together, slept in the same hotels. She never thought anything about it, and no one ever bothered her. Her look said I was a pussy. After a short silence, my boss changed the subject.

About midmorning, one of the other new people, a tall young man came and sat on the edge of my desk. He told me that he knew the two dudes who had worked with the woman who had made the comment. They were extremely grateful that she was gone. They had been terrified the whole time. Subtly, they had tried to get across to her the fact that she wasn't the one in danger. In those cafes and motels they went to, someone could have come in with shotguns and blown them away and nothing would have been done about it. "There wouldn't even have been a serious investigation."

I said that surely she was in danger as well. He said, "No, man, they wouldn't touch a hair on her head. That's the whole point. To let you know that you can't escape being white any more than I can escape being black." He was right, of course. In high school I knew kids who had been pulled over when they were riding around in a mixed crowd. The black kids were dragged out and beaten up. The white kids were only held so that they had to watch.

That semester, two of my fellow graduate students, Luthor and Stephen, decided to go to the poorer part of town and study people's behavior. They were going to simply sit in a bar and observe. Like the traveling young woman, they were dedicated liberals and not afraid. I told them about her, and about leaving town in the middle of a workshop. Luthor said that I was the one who discriminated against minorities. I underestimated their ability to be rational. If confronted by anyone, the two Nordic looking scholars would explain why they were there and how liberal they were. I told them that they underestimated how angry people were. So they went, and Stephen got stabbed in the shoulder by a Latino construction worker. He just casually strode up to their table and stuck him. He never said a word to either of them.

I thought about the fifteen-year-old boy who had told me that he couldn't let me teach, that he couldn't let his classmates forget that just by being white I was part of the problem. I could not change the fact that police would treat me differently—whether I liked it or not. If I hadn't left town, the Klan would almost certainly have treated me much more gently than they would have treated the black teachers in the workshop. I knew that depressed salaries for black and brown colleagues in my own profession would always result in my earning more. My taxes would always be proportionately lower because black and brown labor were paid disproportionately low wages and were forced to take the lousiest jobs.

I thought about the quiet guy, who wanted as much revenge as possible. Maybe he was right. Maybe that was all power could understand. Maybe the establishment had to know that people would rather die than be subjugated. I thought about Lonald, who wasn't really into caste and class struggle, but would always be affected by it. Maybe he was right not to be too aware. Maybe he would find some way to be productive that gave him satisfaction.

I thought about Melanie, who found discrimination incomprehensible and intolerable. She would disagree with the quiet guy and with the fifteen year old and with Lonald. She would feel there was a role for all of us. I thought about Hillary. If Hillary knew what was going on, would she join forces with Melanie? Probably.

That summer I was invited to spend several weeks in a small city several hundred miles from my university. The school district was in the process of integrating, and the superintendent thought it would be a good idea for teachers to have some preparation for this event before classes began in September. We met every day for several hours in a comfortable meeting room. My students were all white women.

Although I proceeded much more slowly and gradually than in the adult education workshop sessions on prejudice, I still aimed to get at their racism and deal with it. I was surprisingly successful. In no time, these teachers were entirely in sympathy with where I was coming from. They agreed that prejudice was outmoded, primitive, inappropriate. After a week, nothing I said, no example I gave, made anyone uncomfortable. I became excited, even thrilled. It appeared that prejudice could, on occasion, be confronted and reversed thorough rational analysis.

The superintendent of this school district had specifically given instructions that at some time during the course the teachers were actually to visit the homes of some of their prospective minority students. I saved this task for the last week. When I assigned it to my enlightened group, I expected some nervousness, even a little anxiety. Mostly, I expected curiosity and enthusiasm. What I got was blank-faced shock followed by stonewall refusal. The kind of hard looks I got from people who walked out of my workshops. When I insisted, on behalf of the superintendent, several finally made the visits. Some lied. I reminded them of what we had talked about, about their enlightenment. They no longer regarded me with affection.

I left town deflated and confused. About fifty miles down the highway, the vice principal of Melanie's school smiled in my head. His lips were moving. I concentrated. They formed the word "humility." I thought about Hillary again, who could afford to be snobbish but wasn't. I knew why she and Melanie together would be powerful stuff. They saw things clearly, felt good about themselves, and were impractical when it came to compromising their values in exchange for status and rewards. Like the vice principal of Melanie's school and the principal of Hillary's school, Melanie and Hillary also didn't go in for self-pity or self-congratulations.

Among my recent students had been a tall, quiet woman. Outwardly she reacted to the visitation assignment the same way the other teachers did; but without conviction, I sensed. However, my awareness of this fact was overwhelmed by my awareness of the hostility coming from everyone else. When she reported to the class, I had a second sharp perception that she only pretended to consider it to be a disgusting ordeal. This time my awareness was dulled by self-pity.

I had overlooked real gold out of disappointment at discovering that what I had been mining was mostly fool's gold. When I told Shula about this experience, she said that I suffered from the disease I wanted to cure. I prejudged people according to my own stereotype of what a racist looked like. I knew that the vice principal of Melanie's school would agree with her. "Racism is a terrible thing," he would say, "and you don't have to go easy on it. But if you don't have clear vision, you aren't worth much to anybody."

Freshmen

Being a teaching assistant meant teaching introductory sociology to freshmen. It didn't take long for me to understand why Claude was popular with his students. Freshmen need a lot of nurturing, and Claude provided more of this than most teachers did. Our neophytes were bright enough and willing enough, but they didn't understand how things work. This was especially true of those from small towns, like Claude himself. The urbanites were a little more sophisticated.

The first time freshmen's special needs became apparent to me was when a movie called "Blowup," with Vanessa Redgrave, came to town. It was avante garde, antiestablishment. Everyone under thirty-five was lining up for it. I wanted to discuss it in class. A show of hands indicated that most of my students had not seen it. Nor did they plan to. I asked why. Were they all old people, only disguised as young people?

Many voices answered me: "Because we don't have time!"

I asked for clarification. Unappreciated Atlases, straining dutifully under massive loads though no one seemed to notice, my students eagerly described how studying filled a freshman's non-class hours. Freshmen rarely went to the student union. They didn't go beer- drinking or to wild parties or basketball games. They didn't attend interesting, funny, controversial, or blatantly outrageous lectures by the many personalities who constantly showed up on our large campus. In short, they took almost no advantage of most of the richness the university offered.

I voiced amazement. I told them they were more like Sisyphuses than Atlases. "Why do you punish yourselves this way?" I shouted at them.

They responded indignantly: Didn't I want them to make good grades? Why was I encouraging them to do things that took time away from studying?

It was hard to think of an answer. I was used to students who put studying last on their list of priorities. I realized that I had a much heavier educational responsibility to these freshmen than I had assumed. Finally I stated, slowly and loudly: "*You can't let going to school interfere with getting an education!*" They stared at me. Not indulgently, like the kids in Melanie's school, who knew I had a lot to learn. In this case, it was the students who were clueless. "What is the main thing you have to do to make good grades?" I asked. A hand went up immediately.

"Study hard."

I shook my head. "Not necessarily," and pointed at another hand.

"Attend class and take good notes."

"This might help," I granted, "but what is "the main thing?" "Do your homework?"

"No!" All hands went down. Their eyes narrowed. This was obviously a trick question. A hand inched up slowly. I raised my eyebrows at it.

"Suck up to the teacher?"

I nodded with approval. "You're getting warmer."

A long-haired student in the back of the class who had his feet draped over the chair in front of him said, "You got to make good grades on tests, any way you can."

I stared at him. Then I looked all around the class. When the pause was about as pregnant as it could get, I shouted, "Absolutely! That's the whole story."

They expected me to continue. The silence gaped. After a while, a blond girl wearing new Levi's got fed up. Angrily, she stated what was obvious. "You can't make good grades on tests if you don't study. Unless you cheat. Are you advising us to cheat?"

"You can't cheat," the well tanned boy next to her observed. "They have computers. They give everybody a different test."

The sprawled-out student said, "People get good grades in high school by sucking up to teachers." A number of students nodded vigorously.

I asked if anyone could think of a time when studying hard actually didn't help.

"If you study the wrong stuff. That's happened to me in geometry."

"What is the right stuff?" I asked.

"The stuff in the book and the stuff in your notes," answered the girl in new Levi's.

"Wrong!" said the sprawled-out guy. "The right stuff to study is what's going to be on the test. Right, prof?"

"One hundred percent," I confirmed.

"But that's ridiculous!" shouted the blond girl, squirming in the Levi's. "How can you know what's going to be on the test if you don't take notes and read the book?"

"Aha!" I stated. "You're asking the right question. Any ideas?"

A round-faced student sitting in the middle of the class waved vigorously. "My brother never took notes. He just studied old tests. He also never studied 'til the night before an exam. He always bragged about how he didn't learn anything in classes and made better grades than most people who learned a lot. Oh yeah, and he sucked up to teachers."

The girl in clean Levi's tried to interrupt, but the successful student's sibling was on a roll, explaining his brother's philosophy that the key to success in college was to figure out what teachers consider important. "Most of the stuff in notes and books is irrelevant. Sucking up helps you find out what a prof is into. They like to brag about their ideas. Also cramming at the last minute, because lots of times they change their minds. Especially young profs."

"What about studying old tests?" I asked.

"Profs ask the same questions year after year. You don't even need notes if you have their old tests."

I asked him if his brother explained why teachers don't change their tests. He responded that they hadn't gone into it that deeply. I asked the class why they thought a teacher might ask the same questions perpetually.

"They're what he thinks is most important." "Because the material's still the same." "Because they're the best questions possible." I told them they weren't even warm.

A young man wearing a jacket and tie and an expression that said a huge light bulb had just gone off in his head said, "Because he's lazy!"

"Absolutely!" I affirmed.

Heavy stares, glares, furrowed brows, narrowed eyes. How could I rationalize this radical, possibly degenerate assertion? From the stage on which I paced, I never stood behind the lectern, I smiled patronizingly down into a mass of innocent but skeptical faces. I reminded them that most people like to have as much leisure time as possible. After they get their important work done, people enjoy being lazy. Contrary to what high school seniors are told, educating students in the university is not important work. Especially not educating undergraduate students such as them. "This is actually a very low-level task."

"That's total bullshit!" a voice roared from the class. The atmosphere clouded with righteous outrage. I allowed it to swirl and fester a while.

"Maybe it should be bullshit," I finally acknowledged, "but unfortunately it's not. Research and publication are what count," I explained. "Only graduate students contribute to this. Professors compete for bright graduate students, who do professors' slave work and are rewarded by being fed driblets of knowledge from time to time. Undergraduates are simply a nuisance to be put up with because they provide the university with needed revenue."

Sober silence now. This was more than outrage. This was sacrilege. Two students walked out. Others looked furious. Most were intrigued. "Some of your teachers spend more time figuring out how not to waste time giving you grades than they spend preparing lessons. Writing good test questions takes a lot of time. They know that using questions over and over is not valid, so they compromise. They throw in a couple of new questions now and then."

"But their questions are hard. You still have to study!" a voice insisted.

"Yeah, but not everything," another voice responded. "If you just memorize old tests you'll make a pretty good grade."

"The way to study is to figure out what we won't ask and concentrate on what we will ask." I continued. "We pretty much stay away from anything the least bit subtle. We don't want you in our offices debating with us all the time. We'll ask questions based on our notes, especially over things we stress, for the same reason. How often do you think most teachers rewrite their notes?"

"Never!" several voices responded. They were beginning to get the picture.

"What about the book? You still have to read the whole book." someone observed.

"Let me answer!" a student was standing up. "They can't ask real detailed questions from the book because everyone would fail and be in their offices complaining. And they can't ask real general questions because there would be too much argument. So they have to ask the most obvious, main things."

"You perceive the pattern!" I affirmed.

"So you're saying," an articulate student interpreted, "that taking all of this into consideration, we should be able to prepare for most tests without studying more than a fraction of the material actually assigned?"

The bell rang.

No one was late for class two days later. A hand went up immediately.

"I want to make sure I've got this right," he consulted his notes like a lawyer. "Last time you said that we don't have to study in order to make good grades?" His pencil poised to record my answer. I wondered how much longer I would be a teaching assistant.

"Certainly not as much as you're doing." I waded in. "Furthermore, I now submit to you that making good grades and learning a lot have nothing to do with each another. How can I make this statement?"

"Yes, how can you?" Clean Levi's was on her feet, outraged. "You shouldn't be teaching! How can you tell us these terrible things? Why don't you teach us about sociology, like you're supposed to?" She had probably never spoken to a teacher this way.

A tall girl with an afro, two rows further back explained, "He is teaching us sociology. He's just not teaching us about it. We're doing it."

I loved this student. her eyes sparkled the way Melanie's did when we began to get at the core of things. Like Melanie, she wasn't afraid to find out how things operate in the real world. I sensed that many in the class were, however. Turning toward me, she continued: "The reason you can make that statement is why my sister always makes better grades than me but never knows as much. She crams and then forgets it. I learn it all and understand it all but don't memorize the trivia."

"Me too," affirmed a thin boy wearing huge glasses. "I never understood it before. Also, if the professor asks the same questions every year and never changes his notes, he's probably not staying up-to-date. So to make a good grade you have to know wrong things and not know right things."

This was a little too radical even for me, but I couldn't deny there was validity in his observation. I stated that now that we had painted an extreme picture—exactly the opposite of what they had all assumed education was—we had to go back and modify it. We had already begun to engage in something called dialectical analysis.

We spent the entire semester doing dialectical analyses of controversial issues and never memorized a single sociological term or concept. And it didn't end with the course. Many of these students came back periodically to report on how they were continuing to dialectically analyze things, driving their parents and others crazy. The sociological analysis of education had helped them make better grades, while not missing out on the opportunity to become worldly, cynical, even moderately degenerate during their crucial formative years at the university.

Part Four

Up East

Social Work

By the time I finished graduate school, in the spring of 1968, and was ready to accept my old friend the dean's offer of a job, he was out. Along with many other departments at his university, the school of social work was undergoing radical change--literally. The president of the university, together with his closest lieutenants, had decided to make it a truly sixties place. They wanted people who identified with students' rights, minority rights, the oppressed. They wanted social and behavioral sciences to be concerned, humanities to be relevant, and natural sciences to be responsible. Most of all, they didn't want academics who lived in an ivory tower. They wanted new blood, even if it meant that old blood must flow. One of the dean's last official acts was to hire me. He expressed no bitterness and told me not to feel any either. This was the future. The old must make way for the new. "Fit in," he told me. "Be a part of it."

Because I arrived before the new regime took over, the people who welcomed me were those members of the social work faculty the dean had hired over the years. Most of them had left active field duty to accept a job training neophytes to the profession. Each of these experts had a unique, rich background. Each had been on the frontlines, and had the scars to prove it. Some had simply burned out and welcomed an academic appointment. They all seemed to have been raised in the same tribe, with its own peculiar set of values. For one thing, they all possessed immense humility. They tried to hide it, but it was obvious to an outsider. I mentioned this one day as five or six of us on the faculty were riding to lunch in Frank's station wagon, during a near blizzard. He was a terrible driver, and I was becoming nauseated and terrified in the back seat. I wanted to start a conversation, to get my mind off of my stomach. I said, "I'm really impressed with how much humility all you social workers have."

"You're full of shit!" they replied in chorus.

"No one is more cynical than us," asserted Frank, a tall man in his forties with huge creases in his face that made him appear perpetually sad. "We are, without doubt, the most cynical bastards alive. Why shouldn't we be?"

"I'm not so sure we're absolutely the most cynical," Dorothy disagreed. The same age as Frank, she had creases too. Hers said she knew how to endure pain. "I think maybe cops are more cynical."

"Not really," observed Stan, ten years younger than Frank and Dorothy, uncreased, whose eyes were deep pools containing things you didn't want to see. "I've known some softhearted cops, but I've yet to meet a softhearted social worker."

"Exactly my point," Frank stomped on the brake for emphasis and skewed left. I couldn't believe no one complained about his driving.

"This discussion," Nick said, grabbing my arm as we leaped into a right turn, "is ridiculously academic. Who cares how we feel? We have no power." Nick, a little younger than Frank and Dorothy, was equal mixtures of outrage and compassion. His eyes sparkled with warmth above a mouth tense and drawn.

"That isn't necessarily true," Dorothy stated deliberately, while we careened into the crowded parking lot of a diner. Since everyone except me was starving, she had to wait for a response until we crowded into the last remaining booth and intensely studied the menu, which they all knew by heart.

They were obsessively dialectical. They debated everything, especially the many things they felt guilty about. They felt guilty about not being able to do more. They felt even guiltier about not being willing to do more. If they worked eighty or ninety hours week after week and finally decided to spend some time relaxing, they felt guilty. They felt guilty about not fighting the establishment harder. They knew when policy was designed to gloss over rather than solve problems. They knew when agency heads stole funds.

"Why do we always feel so powerless? Why do we accept doing so little within the system instead of trying to change the system?" Stan asked me, the supposedly innocent and therefore uncorrupted neophyte.

"Because getting political just gets people isolated," Frank answered him, ignoring me.

"Or unemployed," added Nick.

"So what? Maybe we should do it anyway," said Dorothy, also looking at me as though my opinion mattered.

"Why are we such cowards?" she was directly in my face. She stared at me until my lips parted to speak, then turned to Nick for the answer.

"We're not exactly cowards," he said, "we're real-
ists." "Bullshit!" stated Frank, wiping ice cream off his
chin.

During the terrifying ride back to the university, they didn't resolve anything. They never did.
Their dialectical arguments were therapy, but they
were also a form of genuine agonizing.

At Melanie's school it had not dawned on me until
near the end of my tenure that simply by nonconforming I was expressing dissent. I acted as I felt appropriate and wasn't rehired. Did my actions have real
impact? I wondered now. In any case, I realized, my
situation wasn't really comparable to a social worker's. The consequences of a public school teacher's
nonconforming were clearly not as heavy as the
consequences of the average social workers' failure to
comply. Teachers are not usually faced with the
kinds of terrible system realities confronting social
workers. A social worker observes huge sums being
squandered on the bureaucracy of aid, while being
allowed to offer someone who actually suffers help so
minimal that it tortures both giver and receiver. Yet
this pittance may mean the difference between
someone's starving or not starving, working at slave
labor or not working at all, receiving pitifully inadequate health care, or none at all.

A teacher is not routinely required to place students in jeopardy. Social workers constantly have to
do things that are dangerous for clients. A social
worker is required by law to follow up on a report of
child molestation, knowing with certainty that confronting the parent will cause the child to receive even
worse abuse. The social worker is authorized to
request help from law enforcement but is powerless

to ensure that the police act swiftly, or at all, to remove a child to safety. Clara, a small, tough woman who almost never laughed, but when she did she lit up the world, was the wife of my friend the deposed dean. She worked with infant abuse cases. She examined babies with fresh cigarette burns every time she visited certain families. She hoped against hope that the wheels of bureaucracy would get around to ending their torture before they died.

"If we all get fired for being political," she said, "there won't be anyone to even attempt to treat these pathologies."

"On the other hand," her husband--a tall man bent with years of exhaustion but possessed of the fiercest eyes and the strongest gaze I ever encountered-- argued back, "maybe it would be better to let the victims suffer more, until social outrage becomes so great that real change can occur."

"What outrage?" she shouted. "Our clients are invisible to the public."

"Nevertheless, we must be more political," he insisted "other-wise we are part of the problem ourselves."

The new regime was different. They were young, enthusiastic, and had terrific self-confidence. None of their faces had creases, nor did their eyes express anything but their ambitions. They never second-guessed their own actions or positions about anything. They weren't interested in child abuse per se--they were interested in political action. Although not themselves minority group members, they identified with minorities. They especially identified with minority people who were militant. Although none of these social workers had actually been beaten up by police, they were powerfully sure they understood what it meant to be angry and black or brown in America. Even though none of them had gone hungry or spent much time around anyone who was hungry, they identified completely with people in poverty. They had hungry minority friends who they invited to their parties. I was impressed and somewhat intimidated. Though I had spent more time than any of them close to racism and poverty, I had little of their confidence. I was still trying to figure out how I fit in.

They also knew who was the enemy. They didn't have to study the actual work experiences of the old-timers, or listen to their agonizing, to know that the latter were cowardly prostitutes. To the new regime, anyone was a whore to power if he or she did not actively fight the establishment. This was done by participating in demonstrations and by expressing rhetoric.

One afternoon, during a faculty meeting, Nick suggested that some of the new regime might benefit by actually spending some time in an inner-city ghetto. His field specialty had been organizing inner-city people to fight for city services they were entitled to.

"That isn't necessary," the new dean responded impatiently. A look of tolerant disdain graced his smooth young face. Twelve of us sat around a long table. He was at one end, presumably the head. "We all know what it's like. You people need to stop discussing and start doing. Or else begin thinking about early retirement!"

"Tell me what it's like?" Frank asked softly, from the other end of the table.

"People are out of work, they're poor, the police constantly hassle them. But they're fighting back," one of the new dean's people, an extremely healthy young woman, responded angrily from the other end of the table.

"Which you approve of?" asked Frank.

"Certainly. And we have to help them." She explained patiently, as to a child.

"How?"

"By speaking out, by teaching our students what goes on, by demonstrating." She leaned toward Frank, reaching out, teaching him.

"How about going down there and fighting the way they fight." He gazed straight back into her eyes. "The way you say you applaud them for fighting." Her teaching smile flattened, and her eyes began to blink. "The way you even tell them they ought to fight." His still soft voice had a hard edge. "Live for a while in the ghettos. When the cops come at night, be there to share the reality," She shrank back in her chair and looked at the young dean, whose face was white and drawn.

No one said a thing. Finally Nick asked, "What do you think actually happens at night in the ghettos?"

"They get hassled," another member of the new regime, a nervous owl faced young man, answered impatiently.

"What does that mean?" Nick asked, relentlessly.

"They get pushed around, beaten up," the response was a little high-pitched.

"How badly?" Nick leaned toward him, elbows crossed in front of him, fists clenched.

No answer.

"Why not go down there and get beaten up with them?" Nick slapped the table, and the owl faced man jumped. "Stand up with them?" he shouted. "Actually experience what they experience?" The new Dean tried to take control, but Nick drowned him out. "Maybe the papers will pick up on that: 'White Social Workers Beaten Up in Ghetto.' A good headline might be better than demonstrating."

"Why don't you do it?" the healthy young woman suddenly shouted, almost a shriek, still shrunk back in her chair.

Frank smiled sweetly at her, signaling Nick to subside. "You kidding? I'm scared shitless! I do admire people who risk pain and death going after what they're entitled to. But I don't tell them they ought to -- unless I'm willing to take the risk myself."

Yet both he and Nick had spent time in a hospital for doing precisely that. Neither mentioned this fact.

I was regarded with suspicion by the new dean's people because the old dean had hired me and because I came from south of the Mason-Dixon line. On the other hand, I was the same age as they were, and the new dean seemed to like me–to feel that deep down I might be potentially their kind of radical. One morning he invited me in to his office. He stated candidly that he hoped I'd decide to join his team. He told me I ought to distance myself from the old timers and demonstrate solidarity with his people. Joining them in expressing appropriate rhetoric at faculty meetings, and in classes, would be a step in the right direction.

I visited my friend the deposed dean at home. We sat in beach chairs on a screened-in porch, drinking tea. I told him I thought I should leave the school. He told me not to allow silly chivalry or unnecessary loyalty to stand in the way of building a career. "This new bunch are pretty crass, no question about that, but they aren't entirely wrong."

He made a speech that sounded more determined than heartfelt about the need for more dissent in social work. Social workers didn't have to be as passive as they were, he insisted. He himself had gone along too much with the powers that be. Clara, making marmalade in the kitchen behind us, uttered a loud guffaw.

"Hell, look at my staff. They're all white middle-class," he persisted, leading me out into the yard — to avoid further spousal editing, I supposed.

"Right, because they were trained in schools of social work, which are controlled by the established interests, which favor whites. This is true in every discipline," I defended him.

He nodded, "Especially in social work. Can't have the clients knowing how corrupt the system is. But I could have challenged the status quo. Unattractive as they may be, this new bunch do."

"Give me and you both a break," I challenged him. I had known him since I was a kid. I had heard stories about him from my parents all my life. He was not a coward. "You would have challenged authority more if you thought doing so would be effective."

"You're partly right," he acknowledged. "I operated on the principle that in order to accomplish anything significant as public servants, we would have to work with rather than against those in power. Without becoming dishonest or corrupt we needed to gain their confidence, make them feel comfortable with us. I hoped our role in shaping policy would grow from tokenism to the real thing. We wouldn't get everything we wanted, certainly, but more than we could any other way. Gentle pressure, relentlessly applied."

He paused and rubbed his forehead. He looked tired. He bent down to examine a rose bush. "For a long time I convinced myself that we did enough good to justify not pushing harder. I'm not sure now."

He stood up and faced me directly. "Don't ever imagine that America is a democracy. It's always been an autocracy. I don't worship power, but I accept it as real. Power is powerful."

"Your successor and his bunch don't think so," I pointed out. "They think its a game. They don't have a clue."

"They'll learn," he asserted. "I don't want to discourage them. At this point in my life I see that things are not significantly improving. People like me have had little effect. Power is more rapacious, more cynical, crueler than ever. It has to be challenged. I'm afraid that only people who have no concept of what they're up against will make the effort."

While we were talking, his wife had quietly joined us. "These people are not serious," she said. "They won't last. They're rank opportunists."

The dean said, "Maybe so, but who else have we got?"

I thought about the vice principal at Melanie's school. His options had been much more limited than the dean's. Nevertheless, he would say that it doesn't help to overreact just because you think for a long time you underreacted. On the other hand, he would agree that things don't necessarily improve in the manner you think they ought to.

Police

Teaching social work graduate students about doing behavioral science research was fun. They had no difficulty perceiving the difference between studies that were precise and sterile and studies that had some meat. How to tell when a meaty study was seriously flawed was more difficult. How to design a good meaty study was more difficult still. They rose to the challenge. They knew that the meatier a study was, the less likely it was to arrive at a clear-cut conclusion--and this didn't bother them. The world of social work was filled with vagueness. They had already learned that social workers can't always follow cases through to resolution. Sometime they can't even find out whether a case was ever resolved. The students were resigned to these facts of life. I admired them but knew that I could never be a social worker.

I longed to do some sociology. There is vagueness in sociology too, but it is macro-vagueness rather than micro-vagueness. Worrying about a group is less emotionally stressful than worrying about an individual. When I thought about Melanie and about the vice principal of her school, I thought about them as social beings rather than as individuals. I didn't really know much about their private lives. On the other hand, their social existence was not less actual than their private existence. They had an impact on people around them. Einstein asserted that no mysterious force of gravity exists. Massive bodies simply shape the space they occupy; they make dents in it, causing lesser masses to flow into their dents and orbit around them. Melanie and the vice principal made dents in society.

I had no doubt that the character of society has a huge effect on the health and welfare of the individuals who share it. I found myself thinking about the Meensom boys. I felt certain they were not really evil, even though they behaved evilly. Somehow, evil behavior was normal in the society they grew up in, which was not, somehow, precisely the same as the society I grew up in. If it was, I would feel abnormal for not wanting to behave evilly. But I didn't. Therefore, in my world my attitude was normal, but in their world it would not have been. If I had grown up in their world, people would have thought me strange if I didn't think it would be fun to see some little kid fall to his death.

Maybe the Meensom boys behaved evilly so that people in their society wouldn't think them strange. Maybe being strange was worse than being evil. When Nick, who had been a community organizer, offered to get me included on a large civic project involving police, I accepted eagerly. No one is more immersed in evil than the police, I thought. Maybe I could learn more about it, and about the different kinds of societies that occupy the same space in America.

It was called a human relations project, sponsored by the city council. My section met in a huge room. I stood at the front on a little stage, and the police, all men, sat in straight-back chairs arranged in rows. The purpose of the project was to promote better relations between police and the community. My job was to encourage policemen to talk about their jobs—about how they felt about their jobs and the people they protected.

The officers assigned to me weren't reluctant to talk. It was what they didn't say that surprised me. They didn't say that society was too soft on crime or to easy on criminals, that police brutality was overstressed, or that the bad guys were winning.

"What you gotta understand," explained a tall lanky sergeant, "is the real bad guys aren't the sleazeballs we arrest. The bad guys are the assholes in the Governor's Mansion, and the mayor's office, and the downtown clubs." He counted them off on his fingers. He was referring to those exclusive sanctuaries that exist in every large city, where the very elite meet informally to conduct business that affects everybody. Many heads nodded in agreement.

"Right!" agreed his buddy, who was as broad as the other was tall. They looked like Mutt and Jeff, but I couldn't imagine anyone sharing this observation with them. They also looked tough and dangerous. "Including our own brass. They go along with it."

"Go along with what?" I asked.

"Sweeping shit under the carpet! Crime is OK as long as we keep it out of your neighborhood."

Another officer expanded on this point: "What we're telling you is, our job's nothing like what you see on TV. We aren't really supposed to clean up crime. Just keep it out of sight. Fat cats only care about getting rich. They make a lot of garbage getting rich. Human garbage. They don't worry about that. They make sewers to shove it in. What you nice people call slums, they're the sewers. We're sewer keepers. We keep the losers in the sewers. If they try to get out, we shove them back in."

A freckle faced cop added, "And what do you expect sewers to breed? Rats. Human rats."

I asked about police brutality.

"Sure there's brutality," a burly beat cop admitted. "You give us no way to help these poor bastards. We're just your club to beat 'em down with. Who wants this kind of fucking job? Crazy people. And mean assholes."

I asked if they thought the powers that be could clean up crime if they wanted to.

"Not totally," an officer with a scar along his right cheek admitted. "But they don't make a real effort. They aren't serious about it."

"So why do you guys do it?" I asked. "Why are you still cops?"

"It could be a good job," said a man with a gentle face but hard eyes. "It used to be a good job. The cop on the beat was part of the community. He was a friend. Now he's an enemy."

"OK, hold on. Lot of times, it's still not so bad," the one who looked like Jeff retorted.

"Bullshit!" the one who looked like Mutt responded. "Most of the time it's lousy. Nobody likes or respects us. We're just niggers who keep other niggers in line. Don't matter what color skin you have, you're still a nigger."

Once every two weeks, Nick taught classes at the state prison. It was one of the largest in the country, housing particularly dangerous inmates. There had been bad riots there, with guards taken hostage and killed. Nick didn't seem nervous about going in, but I was--the first time and every time he took me along. It was the first prison I had visited. I was overwhelmed by its oppressiveness.

It began the second I entered the front gate. I knew immediately that if someone screwed up and didn't realize I didn't belong there, there was no way I would get out. I felt that even if there were no guards and no bars, I couldn't get out. Somehow the place itself claimed me. It would have to give me up voluntarily.

While Nick taught the inmates, I observed the guards. How did they feel? Their faces were different from the faces of the cops in the human relations project. The guards faces were washed out. These men were just another category of prisoners. They were paid salaries and could come and go, but the prison had claimed them. It only let them go because it wanted to, not because the state said it had to. I asked some of them if they liked the work. They all said they would leave if they could. They weren't qualified for anything else and their families needed the salary.

I told Nick that the prison seemed less cruel to the prisoners than to their guards. It didn't let them have any dignity and it didn't let them escape. It had no respect for the fact that their own decency, their sense of responsibility to their families kept them bound. He said there was more to it than that. "Everybody needs something to do, someplace to belong. The guards believe this is it. Most of the prisoners don't believe that."

Even the long road back to the city was dreary. Neither of us said anything for a while. Then he added, "Some of the guards are sadistic and some are just passive. I'm not sure who's more fucked up."

Foremen

Nick, my colleague who was who got hospitalized because he hung out with the wrong people at the wrong time in the inner city instead of judiciously inviting them to a party in the suburbs, could not stop organizing. He networked with friends in companies and institutions all over the state. As a result, he got his students the best job placements of anyone. He also got himself and selected others all kinds of extra jobs, like working on the police human relations project. The next thing he included me in on was a business school workshop being run for a large corporation. This workshop was one of many being conducted simultaneously at universities all over the country.

The purpose of this massive project was to train different groups of personnel within the corporation in special areas. One of these groups consisted of foreman-level workers, and one of the specialized areas they needed training in involved something I was familiar with. The corporation wanted to broaden their ethnic horizons. This corporation was known for hiring high-quality people, and the foremen were no exception. However, most of them had no more than a high school education. In addition, they were mostly white, Anglo-Saxon, and Protestant. The people who worked under them were mostly not. The company wanted the foremen to drop words like "nigger," "spic," and "greaser" from their vocabulary.

I got the picture. I was to do pretty much the same sort of thing I did in graduate school working for the adult basic education program. It looked like easy money. I started out the way I always started out, talking about prejudice in general terms, indicating that it was not necessarily something negative. We met in c classroom in the Business School, and the foremen sat in desks with arms, like ordinary university students. They did not seem the least bit nervous. They didn't look down or away. They looked straight at me. When I asked for an example of "good" prejudice, a hand went up immediately.

"Hating niggers."

"And spics," another voice added. There were about twenty of them, all looking at me blank-faced. Nobody cracked a smile.

"And kikes," offered a third.

I restrained my immediate impulse and tried to get back on track. I asked them if there was any sort of prejudice they could think of that didn't involve hating someone. No response. No hand budged from its lap. No one even coughed. When I realized there wasn't going to be any response, I gave an example. Then I gave another. I stretched out giving examples to the point of absurdity. Then I dismissed them early. There was no way I was going to introduce the psychology of racism until I had a chance to talk to someone in charge. I imagined the next session turning into a riot.

I was sitting in the empty room trying to figure out how I should have started out with this group when someone came in and sat in the chair next to me. I wasn't even aware of his presence until he started speaking.

"They didn't tell you what to expect, did they?" he said.

I couldn't help staring at him. He was in his middle thirties, tall, handsome in a way both rugged and refined, and wore a full-length mink overcoat. He was in charge of the workshop. In fact, he was in charge of all the workshops. He explained to me that this was an experiment. The corporation was debating whether to start its own school or to continue using specialized people from universities. He said that the foremen had not been told anything about how this workshop would be conducted. Its purpose was to open them up to new ideas. They were tough guys, used to being treated in a direct manner. I didn't need to be gentle with them.

"I was watching you from out in the hall. You wanted to shove it down their throats. Do it!" he said, banging his fist on the desk with a big smile. "They can take it."

I told him it could get pretty rough. Some of them might lose their tempers. He said not to worry about it. They might get angry but they had good self-control. He had confidence in his people. "Take off the kid gloves and let 'em have it."

I still wasn't sure how I would begin the next session. I didn't have to worry--one of the foremen raised his hand immediately.

"Say, you're a Jew, aren't you?" "Yeah, I'm Jewish," I answered.

"Would it bother you if I refer to you as a kike?" "I guess not. If I can call you a redneck." Chuckles all around.

"So tell me, how come all you kikes are nigger lovers?" he continued.

I said, "I don't just love niggers, I also love spics, greasers, dagos, and just about everybody but rednecks."

Real laughter. A different voice asked, "What do you have against rednecks?"

"Rednecks tend to be sociopaths," I responded mildly. No laughter.

"What the fuck do you mean by that?"

"If you really want to know, it's going to take a while."

Pretty much as I had done with Melanie's class and the white teachers of black Basic Education students, I explored the social psychology of racism. I asked questions which they made no effort to answer, and then answered them myself.

Why does one need other people to hate? Because one feels inadequate. Because one is inadequate. Because the people one runs around with feel, or are, inadequate and will persecute one if one doesn't show solidarity.

Don't lower-class whites in America have good reason to feel inadequate? They are part of a class, rather than a caste, system. Therefore, the possibility of upward mobility exists for them, if they're tough and smart. Isn't it obvious that those who don't move upward are not as tough and smart as those who do? Black and brown people, on the other hand, are lower caste people. They are denied upward mobility even if they are tough and smart. Therefore, doesn't it stand to reason that a lot of poor black and brown people must be smarter and tougher than a lot of poor white people?

Do white people admit that they fear competing with minority people? Of course not. They make excuses to justify denying them the American dream that whites themselves supposedly believe in. These excuses are so thin that a person would have to be either really dumb or crazy to believe in them. Most rednecks are not that dumb. So they have to become crazy to justify the violence they preach and practice.

Is this craziness harmful to the crazy person? You bet. It justifies the cruelties of racism, but it also entrenches it as an excuse for failure. Psychologists observe that white people from poor backgrounds continue to feel inadequate even when they get ahead.

Where Melanie and her classmates had been electrified with the enlightenment this analysis afforded, the foremen were painfully jolted by it. However, nobody walked out. They even participated. The man in the mink overcoat had been right. They possessed self-control and were smart. They picked every point to pieces. They attacked my conclusions and gave examples of white victimization, both on and off the job. At the end they came by individually and thanked me for doing a good job.

"Things you said were hard to listen to. You really pissed people off. But you did what you were supposed to. We appreciate that."

Talking about the psychopathology of racism and overcoming it are different things. I had had that lesson reinforced already. I mentioned my concerns when the man in mink approached me the last night of the workshop and told me the corporation was going to start its own school and would like to hire me, at about double my present salary. I asked if my job would include helping to discover and reinforce foremen who did not need to be racist, and finding other jobs for those who did. Because that was what it would take.

He stated candidly that the corporation was not much concerned about whether the foremen were racist or not. It wanted them to stop overtly acting in a racist fashion. In time, changing their behavior might change their attitudes.

I asked Nick what he thought. He said, "Take the job. You'll never get a better offer."

I asked him if he thought the corporation was committed to creating a more enlightened and egalitarian workforce.

He laughed. "They're only concerned about their public image. They don't give a shit about minority workers."

I thought about Melanie and third-period class. I thought about the vice principal of Melanie's school and the principal of Hillary's school. In my mind they were silent. Neither advised me to be pragmatic for once--to take the job. But they didn't advise me not to, either. Even my old friend the fired dean didn't offer an opinion. The factor that tipped the scales was the weather. It never stopped snowing. We were living in a tiny house, and every time Shula got our daughters into snowsuits they had to pee. She said, "Tell everybody to go fuck themselves. Let's go where it's warm."

Part Five

Back Home

Jack

One of my former professors had written to me about a sociology position he wanted to recommend me for. He thought this department, a few hours drive from my alma mater, would be pretty receptive to someone more interested in teaching and working in the community than publishing journal articles. Their university was going through a kind of rebirth in the early seventies. Historically a conservative city university, recently it had become part of the state system. Expansion was making it more liberal. An entirely new administration had swept the old guard out on their asses, which is how things were done in both the state and the city where this school was located. They invited me for an interview, which resulted in an offer.

Meanwhile, a good friend at the university that still employed me was urging me to stay there. He was pretty sure he could get me into his department—sociology—and out of the war-torn school of social work. This was a career opportunity not to be taken lightly. The department of sociology at this university was prestigious. I was wavering. The weather stepped in again and decided the issue: a blast of cold air hit us in the face when we opened our front door on the last day of May. We were in shorts and bathing suits heading for the park. This was the last straw. My Southern, and Shula's Mediterranean fascination with winter in this city had already evaporated, when we watched our lovely first real snowfall ever turn black with industrial soot almost overnight. It stayed that way for months, until a thaw and another fresh snowfall that became immediately grungy. The new job was in a tropical place.

My former professor had told me when I got down there to make a special effort to get to know a particular member of the department: Jack. Among my mostly warm and welcoming new colleagues, Jack alone was completely disinterested in me. He didn't want to know where I had been or what I had done. He was polite but apparently wrote me off as a typical product of early sixties sociology graduate schools: bright-eyed, bushy-tailed, possibly well-meaning, one-dimensional—either someone who wanted to find things to quantify or, worse still, someone who wanted to change things without any real grasp of what needed changing, or why.

I perceived him, on the other hand, to be the kind of person I most wanted to know. He was brilliant and incisive. He didn't care about convention. His totally white middle class family lived in a completely black mixed-class neighborhood—mostly to save money, he insisted, and because it was close to work. He was utterly unprejudiced. He had little use for anyone, except his students and his family and a few friends.

One day he was walking around the sociology department with a particularly pained look on his face. He was thin, medium tall, in his forties, walked with a slight stoop and always looked distressed anyway, but today he looked more distressed than usual. I asked him what was wrong. Without looking at me or breaking stride he muttered that his hemorrhoids were driving him crazy. A few days later he was crossing campus between classes, about fifty yards from me. Campus wasn't crowded—it was the end of summer—but there were quite a few people around. I yelled, "Hey Jack! How's your asshole?" His mouth fell open. I never saw that happen again during all the time I knew him.

He smiled and said, "Better, thanks." During the following weeks we became close friends.

Jack was an anomaly in the department and in sociology. Widely considered one of the best writers in the profession he was disinterested in publishing. He felt it was a waste of time. All who came in contact with him, including those who hated him, were overwhelmed by the power of his intellect and somehow he survived. Nevertheless, his students worried about him. One Friday night, after midnight, a group of them knocked on his door wanting to speak to Dorothy, Jack's wife. They had been partying and at a certain stoned point in the evening the solution to Jack's problem came to them. Someone needed to lock him in his bathroom until he slid pages of manuscript under the door, just as Zelda Fitzgerald had done to F. Scott. Dorothy was a gentle, practical woman who was also very pretty. She said with a grin that she wanted to stay good looking, and told them that they'd have to find someone else to lock Jack up.

At the time Jack was interviewed, everyone in the sociology department hated teaching theory and were delighted when this was his exact aim. If some of his colleagues had a hint of what this would mean for the department and the university, they said nothing, and the degree of Jack's sophistication was beyond the experience of university administration. They had no conception how radical he was. They thought he was merely eccentric, which they actually liked. It made him seem more professorial. Before they realized who he really was, he was as ensconced as a rattlesnake in a rat hole.

Jack's sociology combined C. Wright Mills and Thorstein Veblen. He had no use for studies that were mathematically precise but didn't make any sort of common sense, and he understood economic theory perfectly. In most sociology classes, students studied things as presented—how established institutions set policy and ran things, for example. In Jack's classes, nothing was taken for granted. His students were never allowed to accept the locus of power as given. They had to determine where it was—objectively. "How much power does the president really have?" he would begin a class.

Jack's students were not allowed to accept government or industry statements of policy intention at face value. "The Fed says it's raising interest rates to halt runaway inflation. Shall we merely nod our heads in appreciation, or drop our trousers, bend over, grab our ankles, and apply Vaseline as well?"

Jack's students had to analyze policy outcomes and then trace backward to get at their purpose. He would ask them, for example, "Was the sorry fate of the freed slaves merely an unfortunate accident? Or was this predictable?"

If they discovered disturbing gaps between what they had been told all their lives and what they now began to perceive as real, Jack's students were forced to delve into these discrepancies. If Lincoln's concern about slavery wasn't as pure as the driven snow, then what was it as pure as? If the government wasn't as wholeheartedly dedicated to trying to get people back to work as it claimed, then what did it aggressively pursue? "If the president of our great republic isn't the powerful sonofabitch that everybody thinks he is, then who actually is?" This was real sociology, strong stuff. Students had to formulate plausible arguments. They learned to regret being sloppy, because Jack had a switchblade-sharp tongue and a wit as dry as a plastic nipple. They could expect no pity. They developed respect for good thinking. They learned to discover things that were hidden. All became intellectual detectives. Some became political activists as well.

Serious students loved Jack. Dilettantes who didn't have the stomach or imagination to read and argue avoided him like the plague. Most of his colleagues in the sociology department didn't understand him. Moreover, Jack made them nervous. Administration watched him like a hawk. After the backlash, many from both groups feared and loathed him.

For a short time, during the year I was hired, Jack actually became more or less mainstream. Along with me, some forty-five other people were hired during the university's rebirth transition, many in the social and behavioral sciences. All of us were more like Jack than like the old faculty. He was widely sought after and admired. Jack was mostly disgusted by his new status, especially when deans and vice presidents spoke warmly to him in passing. He assumed it was some kind of fad. As things turned out, it was. The nationwide reaction to sixties student radicalism was already inflicting heavy casualties on the university that had previously employed me. It hit this school exactly one year later. The old regime swept out their usurpers just as neatly as the latter had removed the old regime. Only a few of those hired during the rebirth remained. I wasn't one of them, and Jack became persona non grata again.

The sociology department changed forever during the university's brief rebirth renaissance. Before the renaissance, most department members had avoided controversial topics, such as how power really works in society. After the renaissance, following the backlash, they embraced such subjects, but in a rarified academic way that rendered them meaningless. Before the renaissance, Jack had been criticized for analyzing power radically. Afterward, he was criticized for not quantifying the variables which comprised power. Jack explained to his students that in the new sociology, being scientific was more important than being scholarly. This meant measuring and quantifying everything. One of his academic friends summed up the affect of the renaissance upon Jack. Before it he was merely a gadfly. After it, he became a menace.

The renaissance had a profound effect upon the student body. Suddenly not just Jack's, and a few other professors' students awoke. They all awoke, all across the campus, invigorated like flowers fertilized for the first time ever. The student newspaper started publishing irreverent articles. Students challenged university curricula and public policy. They remonstrated and demonstrated. Things quickly got out of hand.

In sociology, the very hotbed of student dissent, our efficient, pleasant mannered chairperson was swept aside in favor of a new tougher department head. This was a person with national status—a short, severe looking man with a full head of white hair. He brought in faculty who were dedicated to quantitative science but could talk the talk of the sixties. He considered himself a polished diplomat. He told us that he intended to avoid conflict without appearing unresponsive. Rather than confront graduate students, who now demanded to be included in the design of departmental policy that affected them, he threw crumbs. One crumb was to allow a few students to attend faculty meetings as observers. They could not participate in meetings but following a meeting they could submit any inputs they had in writing. These inputs, he assured them sincerely, would be taken seriously. The students, not fooled for an instant, nevertheless submitted eloquent inputs, which were consistently ignored.

Sociology graduate students played by the new chairman's rules and the student newspaper began to publish well written articles describing the sham of democratic process taking place in Sociology. The paper also documented sociology students' formal and polite request to interview prospective new faculty, and the chairman's non-response. The latter abandoned diplomacy, volubly fuming and threatening, but finally gave in. He closeted himself with interviewees before allowing them to meet with either faculty or students, and coached them not to be drawn into controversy. Students protested that their prospective professors wouldn't deal with real issues and the student newspaper printed more, sometimes brilliant, sociological analyses of the department and the university. Vice presidents and deans no longer smiled at Jack. They held him responsible.

The new chairman ran his fingers through his thick white hair and was clearly not happy. He glared accusations unabashedly, mainly at Jack but also at me, and made it clear that he was far from defeated. He was considered to be tough and he was tough. He was bringing in someone to neutralize Jack's influence. This person turned out to be a sociologist he had worked with in the past, a man who specialized in the study of youth culture. Jack had met him. All Jack would tell me was that he was far more personable than the chairman, who undoubtedly hoped that his friend could heal the rift with students. The chairman would probably make this fellow his assistant. I stared at Jack, waiting for more, but he only grinned, evilly.

At his interview with faculty, the first thing the youth specialist did was insist that students be allowed to participate in the process. The chairman began to protest but the specialist, his friend, placed his arm on the chairman's shoulder and whispered something in his ear, and the latter acceded. The few students who had come to observe and take notes quickly rounded up enough of their peers to fill the meeting room. The specialist began by expressing heartfelt sympathy with students' dissatisfactions. He had a kind, sensitive face, wavy black hair and eyes that seemed to look deeply into a person. He showed as well as said that he identified with young people. He spoke well, exuding charm.

The young people began to listen to him with interest. He drew them out. He rapped with them, and they responded. The atmosphere became positively friendly. No faculty member intervened. The chairman looked actually happy. I glanced sideways at Jack, who sat staring at the table as he usually did during faculty meetings, apparently oblivious. However, a moment later, during a relaxed pause in this interview which was more like a conversation, Jack's deep quiet voice asked, he had not even looked up, "What is your opinion of Rock?"

The laid-back candidate turned to Jack, glancing at the students. He was not the least bit threatened. His eyes sparkled with readiness and fun. Gently, politely, humbly but with a stiletto like sarcastic nuance, he told Jack that he felt humbled in his presence. He said that he was aware of Jack's reputation among the student body and accepted being put on the spot as part of the interview process — to which he had come in good faith, and paused, allowing everyone to decide for himself if anyone present might not be acting in good faith. He admitted that he wanted to make a good impression, and smiled broadly at the students. I almost thought he might wink. Then he turned back to Jack. He placed his elbows on the table and his chin in his hands, and implored Jack please to forgive his terrible memory, and his inability to compete with Jack's immense fund of theoretical knowledge. He himself was a simple scholar, more an agent of change than a student of it, and would appreciate it if Jack could elaborate a little for him.

No one said a word. The chairman's happy look faded several degrees, and a hint of anxiety crinkled the corners of his eyes. The youth expert glanced at the students and returned his steady gaze to Jack. I felt I could read his thoughts. He had read the expressions of amazement upon the students' faces as outrage at Jack's rudeness, the same rudeness they had been accustomed to worship and applaud, but no longer. He had already won them over. Bearding this lion of sociology, this Jack, would be much easier than he had expected.

The lion simply looked confused, and said, "What I mean is, do you feel that rock has had a significant impact on youth culture, especially on the counterculture? Or do you think rock's influence is overrated?"

Now the youth expert and social change agent leaned back in his chair and regarded Jack for a very long moment. His eyes were still warm, but had a certain severe, serious look, which he deliberately shared with the students. He turned to his friend the chairman, whose face registered alarm, and smiled at him reassuringly. Finally, he turned back to Jack. "Jack, I know you have been a hero to some around here," he said, "but perhaps you are also a bully. I am simply not going to play your game or allow you to intimidate me. I know who I am and what I stand for. Therefore, Jack, I'm going to tell you honestly that I don't know who the hell you're talking about. Rock who? Jack."

The chairman buried his face in his hands, Jack looked completely amazed, the students simply walked out. The youth specialist was hired anyway, and things went downhill from there.

Shula and I took our two daughters to visit their Israeli grandparents the summer following my first full year on the new job. I was scheduled to teach the second summer session, but it was going to be difficult to get back on time. I wrote to Jack for help and he offered warmly, which should have worried me, to take my classes for the first couple of days.

We arrived back on a Tuesday night, exhausted. Jack called about midnight, just as we were falling asleep. He told me it might be a good idea if I stopped by his house before going to class Wednesday morning. The class was at 8:30 so I peevishly agreed to be at his place at 7:45. I needed some sleep. He said I'd better make it a little earlier, around 6:45. I told him how much I appreciated all his help, but that he was crazy. He said that I shouldn't be alarmed, but he needed to prepare me for the class. He'd done a little experiment with them.

I slept poorly and got to his house at 6:15, wishing I might be early enough to bang on his door and wake him up—except that I would also wake Dorothy, who was a nice person. It was a moot issue in any case. Jack always got up around 5:30. He made me bacon and eggs, which I love, and explained, as my stomach became so tight that I couldn't eat, what he had done with my class that necessitated this early morning meeting.

The first thing he did was have his crew cut trimmed even shorter than usual. He always wore a crew cut, which on top of his lined, never smiling face made him look like a Nazi. His regular session students teased him about this, but he said it was his disguise. Now that I focused on his appearance, I could see that he might appear quite ominous to most ordinary people who didn't know him. Summer school classes were attended by a different population of student than attended regular sessions. They were mostly older, part-time students trying to put some credits together while working full-time—definitely ordinary people. Many were nurses, teachers, firefighters, etc. None of them were likely to have recognized Jack, or to know much about him even if they did.

Jack told my students that their regular teacher was still out on an assignment. He didn't say, but strongly implied, that I worked for a governmental agency with three letters. He then informed them that I required all students to sign a loyalty oath. He paused to let this sink in. There had been some laughter, a lot of it nervous, and when he didn't smile it died down quickly. He held up the oath and announced that he would distribute it forthwith, unless there were questions. Five students walked out. The rest of the thirty-five enrolled in the class sat mute. Jack distributed the oath, and all but three signed it.

Next day when the class assembled, Jack leaned on the lectern and stared at them for several minutes as they sat in blank faced silence. Then he debriefed them. He told them that they had submitted to the kind of intimidation that American citizens were supposed to be free from. Why had so few challenged the appropriateness of a professor's asking a university class to sign a loyalty oath? "Think about it!" he said, "Your regular teacher will be back tomorrow," and walked out the door.

My head was pounding. I asked about the ones who had not cooperated. He said that a couple of our graduate students had waited outside the classroom and debriefed them as they emerged. He reassured me that no one had dropped the class, yet. I cursed him softly and went to class. I never saw a brighter twinkle in his eye as he smiled me out the door. It was his revenge on me for still being an upper-middle-class white boy who had never really been in deep shit.

It wasn't easy to convince the students that I wasn't a government agent after all. This was their main concern. They were not all that shocked that someone in control had abridged the Bill of Rights. It turned out that most of them took the idea of personal freedom with a grain of salt. They didn't really believe that the United States was a democracy. They didn't mind that it wasn't. Power was powerful, and you had better conform. We spent the entire summer session discussing these things. It was one of the most productive classes I ever had.

One afternoon early that same summer, in Jack's disheveled backyard, where he kept a miserable-looking boat he was supposedly rebuilding, I told him about my old friend the deposed social work dean and his ambivalence about whether the powers that be can be successfully challenged. I had come to the conclusion that he had, in fact, lacked a certain resolve. Jack listened but didn't say anything at the time. Toward the end of the summer I asked him again what he thought. He told me that he basically agreed with me. Then he said that in spite of my efforts to be fair to everyone, I did tend to be a little arrogant. "People aren't insensitive just because they're not as articulate as you. White students and young white professors from well-off families can still fight power in this country without risking too much. For everybody else, there's a lot at stake. If you want people to join a cause, you'd better understand what is at stake for them and not judge them for being afraid."

What Jack said pissed me off. I felt he was right. I stared at an ugly spot on his boat that he had patched but not yet sanded and varnished, and told him that even if I didn't understand things as well as I thought I did, I hoped he would permit me to entertain the conviction that people could take action to make things better. "Things are not totally hopeless," I muttered.

I followed Jack back in the house. Dorothy usually made us lunch but she had gone shopping. Jack began to make bacon and eggs. He taught me how to spoon hot grease on top of the eggs so that you didn't have to turn them over—a lazy dish that my daughters came to love and would never believe their daddy had not invented. After we had eaten, while we were washing our dishes, Jack said that he also didn't think things were hopeless yet, but he wasn't so sure about it.

Existential Sociology

In spite of my professors' efforts to the contrary, graduate school left me unable to teach students that sociology constitutes a body of tried and true scientific knowledge or successfully applies scientific methodology as defined by real (natural) scientists. On the other hand, I also could not bring myself to tell them right off the bat that most of published sociology is sheer pretense at best, and misleading at worst. At some deep level I believed—and still believe—that however questionable sociology's birthright and however brazenly the powers that be manipulate it, sociology's ideal of trying to understand things about human society systematically constitutes an ambitious and admirable dream. At the core of its being, I believe, sociology wants to create useful understandings of important things—the kinds of understandings that change individual lives and human history. It wants to be down-to-earth, not merely philosophical or poetic, although not so grounded in hard fact that it denigrates philosophy and poetry. It wants to be essential, but mainly it wants to be existential.

Once again, I decided to engage my students at actually *doing* sociology before *learning about* the accumulated knowledge of sociology. This way they could see for themselves what was involved. In introductory sociology, for example, I didn't require a specific text. For the first few weeks I probed the class to discover their interests, and assigned books that addressed these. I also compiled a list of topics for discussion, based on their own priorities. It turned out that first on the list was abortion.

About half the class favored legalized abortion and half were against it. I encouraged them to express their views, to argue, to become excited. After ten minutes or so I selected a pair of students who seemed particularly vocal and asked if they would mind debating before the class. They accepted willingly and without hesitation went at it, claw and fang.

"Abortion is murder!" stated the husky young man.

"Abortion is a woman's right to choose!" replied the willowy young woman.

"She shouldn't have gotten pregnant in the first place!" judged he. "What if she was raped?" challenged she.

"What was she doing that got her raped?" he glared. "What if it was incest?" she glared back.

"Only God can decide who lives and dies," he stated pompously. "What if she was incestuously raped and has no money and no job? She can't even feed herself," she asked pleasantly.

"Some people live like animals. No family values, no work ethic," he changed the subject.

"So you want more of them?" she asked ironically.

"Maybe God has something in mind for them?" said he knowingly.

"Like what?" she asked, incredulous. "Who knows?" he answered mysteriously. "Mass extermination?" she asked amazed.

"Who knows?" he answered implying "maybe."

After five minutes I halted the debate and instructed the debaters to switch sides. They stared at me uncomprehending. I repeated the instruction, "You take her position, and you take his."

"I can't," they both insisted, utterly bewildered. "I don't believe in her/his position!"

"So what?" I asked. I turned to the class: "So what? Who can tell me?"

I waited and waited, but no one could. Finally, I explained that the difference between expressing opinions about legalizing abortion and trying to understand it as an issue is the difference between being an ordinary person and being a sociologist. Sociologists are obliged to try to understand things they feel strongly about. Strong feelings are useful because they motivate interest, stimulate ideas, direct thought. However, emotion must not control analysis. One must use one's subjectivity without being governed by it. One way to learn this skill, which is also an art, is to take a position precisely opposite to that which one holds strongly.

"Why would anyone want to do that?" asked a belligerent blond athletic young woman. "What possible value is there in betraying your ideals?"

"I can answer that," a tall young black man replied. "I want to be a lawyer. I'll have to know how my opponent is going to argue. The more I get into his head, the better I'll be prepared."

Everyone agreed with this argument, but only a few students became adept at debating positions they did not hold. Invariably, however, their efforts carried the debaters and their classmates to depths of analysis they had never reached before, and an awareness of connections they had never dreamed were relevant. In the end, they all agreed that sociology had some value.

Most of the time it wasn't difficult to involve students in doing sociology. There were plenty of controversial issues. On two occasions, however, extreme measures were required to get things started. One semester, students in the introductory class all seemed unaware that they lived in a world full of events outside of their own apparently dull perspective. No one, apparently, was touched by any social issue. Compiling a reading list was virtually impossible. On a scale of 1 to 10, the topic that interested any of them the most ranked 2. I became desperate. I stayed awake nights. One morning, as I hunkered before them over my lectern, about to make my ninth or tenth pitch, a perverse idea occurred to me. I would simply tell them about what had happened to me that morning when I came to school — an experience that still frustrated me, and ask what they thought it meant.

I had arisen too late on this particular morning to follow my usual schedule, which included reading the paper while on the toilet. This deviation from routine bothered my digestive system. By the time I arrived at school I needed to go really badly. I headed for the nearest restroom, which was in the building next to my assigned parking lot. I opened the first stall. The toilet seat had been peed on. I checked out the second stall. Same thing. All of the toilet seats in the bathroom had been peed on! "Childish and disgusting!" I thought, and hurried to the next building. Incredible as it seemed, the same condition existed there. In a third building, again all seats peed on. Finally I couldn't wait any longer. I cleaned off a seat as best I could, and did what I had to do.

I asked the class what they thought this experience indicated. A number of people were smiling. Others looked disgusted. Some looked shocked. Hope stirred in my breast. I forged on. There were, I submitted, only two possibilities: either I had been witness to an incredible coincidence or someone—or ones—had systematically befouled a lot of toilet seats. In the latter event, one had to wonder if this indicated a phenomenon only of interest to a psychologist or if there might be something here to merit sociological attention. What did they think?

Fully expecting only silence, I found myself awash in response. They couldn't wait to offer hypotheses and debate one another's reasoning:

It was simply crass, childish, but normal, misbehavior.

It was righteous vengeance upon a heartless bureaucracy. It was the result of deep-seated alienation.

It was because of poor family training. It was due to peer influence.

It could be explained by theories . . .

. . . of social stratification

. . . of individual psychology

. . . of cultural anthropology.

Broad issues of social policy were involved.

The students of that class, once awakened, never faltered in their quest to unravel this bathroom mystery, which ultimately led to exploration of most of the usual subject matter of introductory sociology. They regretted as much as I did the course's conclusion at the end of the semester.

The second class that was unresponsive didn't even blink when I told the toilet seat story. It was a summer school crowd who, except for a few younger students, seemed even more exhausted than summer school students usually were. One afternoon, in response to my most recent effort to stimulate discussion, one of the younger students said, under his breath, but still audibly, "Who gives a shit?" Out of the corner of my eye, I noticed that the attractive middle-aged woman wearing a brightly colored scarf, sitting on the last seat to my right on the front row, visibly flinched. Everyone else remained catatonic.

I walked over to her and asked, "Did that word bother you?" "What word?" she asked. Then added quickly, "No, it didn't bother me, but you don't need to repeat it."

I said, "But if the word 'shit' doesn't bother you, why shouldn't I repeat it?" She flinched again.

"I just don't think it's necessary to use those words," she said. "You can say the same thing using other words."

I paced around the classroom, thinking, and wound up in front of her chair again. "How about the expression 'fucked over' when someone really takes advantage of you?" I asked her. "Is there a satisfactory substitute for 'fucked over'?" She flinched strongly every time the unnecessary word was uttered.

"Why not say, 'badly mistreated,'" she suggested. "It gets the same message across."

I asked the other students, who were suddenly alive, if they agreed that "badly mistreated" was a satisfactory substitute for "fucked over."

About half did. About half didn't. They debated the question for the rest of the period. The following period, and all of the periods that followed for most of the six weeks, we analyzed and debated the sociopolitical implications of rendering certain words forbidden and therefore radical—especially words that happened to have both erotic and aggressive connotations. Exactly as the question of peed on toilet seats had done, this topic too took us deeply into the subject matter of sociology. The woman who had flinched continued to flinch and never uttered a highly charged word. However, she joined actively in discussions and concluded that she might be wrong in thinking that the use of highly charged words wasn't an essential freedom in a healthy society.

About halfway through each semester, invariably, an introductory class student, usually a freshman, would ask me what satisfaction I took out of analyzing everything. This generally occurred at the point when I began gently forcing students to do more analysis of their own. They had enjoyed watching me do it, following my reasoning, sharing my insights. It was less fun to do it themselves. It upset their equanimity, and was difficult. So I would be asked why I did it, what possible enjoyment came from seeing the worst in everything, and why, for God's sake, I wanted them to do it. I got paid for it, after all—they didn't!

I would think of Melanie and respond, at some length, that it wasn't necessary to wear rose-colored glasses in order to find positive value in mortal existence. Reality might be unpleasant sometimes.

However, clear vision opened up new horizons, vistas unatainable without undergoing the pain of discovery. Etc., etc. It was an effective speech and got better the more I did it. One semester, however, perversity again rose up from beneath my lectern and took me hostage.

My inquisitor on this occasion was a particularly wholesome, cheerleader-pretty freshman girl. She had just asked the invariable question. Her brow was creased. The class numbered about two hundred and met in an auditorium. She sat nearly dead center. I started to give my usual response when it happened. I stopped and stared at her and she stared back, quizzically. Our pause lengthened and became pregnant. Then I found myself saying, "Actually, this is not what I would prefer to be doing. This is not my dream."

She responded instantly, "What is your dream?"

"You wouldn't really want to know. It's just my private dream," I couldn't stop myself.

"No really, we do want to know." Her face radiated sincere interest and concern.

"Are you sure you really want to know?" I asked beseechingly. "Oh yes, truly. Please tell me." She leaned forward in her seat.

Her expression was definitely maternal.

"The fact is," I mumbled hesitantly, looking at the floor "there is a profession I have always admired." I looked at her tentatively. "There is something I have always wanted to be but felt inadequate to strive for. I have never told anyone of this desire."

"Go on," she said. She was on her feet now.

I hesitated. The atmosphere was charged. Everyone was caught up in our private dialogue.

"Go on. You can tell me," she urged.

Finally I blurted it out. "The fact is, I always wanted to be a pimp. I want to wear those fancy open shirts. I want to wear high-heeled boots. I want to carry a razor-sharp comb in my back pocket." My voice rose and my eyes blazed. "I want to walk like this," strutting around the stage, demonstrating. I went on and on, continuing even after the class's laughter totally drowned me out. I was still ranting when the bell rang.

My would-be confessor turned out to be made of stronger stuff than I imagined. She didn't drop the course, and when I publicly apologized to her at the beginning of the next period, said, "Don't worry about it. You're a typical fucking male pig. You can't help it!"

The Student with Connections

A student in the class I told I wanted to be a pimp turned out to have serious connections. Following my outrageous admission, I had stayed in character—glorifying sexism, classism, religious purity, ethnocentrism, and racism. This delighted several young men dressed in cowboy hats and boots. The former they never removed and the latter they thrust out over the seats in front of them. Their approval didn't last long. Within a few weeks, all but one dropped the class. One day, a delicate blond young woman, who reminded me of Hillary, raised her hand and asked, "Would you be interested in having some guest lecturers?"

"Such as whom?" I queried.

"The Ku Klux Klan? The Black Panthers?"

"You can get the KKK and the Black Panthers?" I was surprised and cautiously excited.

"I can get them. Are you interested?"

Wondering exactly who this student was, I asked the class. All one hundred plus of them were extremely interested.

"OK," I said, "but on one condition. They have to leave plenty of time for questions and reactions. They have to be willing to interact with the class."

"No problem," she said. "They love that."

"Why would the KKK want us to fire at them?" an incredulous student asked. "Don't they realize most of us think they're disgusting slime?"

"They eat up conflict," she responded. "You don't realize. They wouldn't be doing us a favor; we would be doing them a favor. They welcome any opportunity to get before a large group. Laying their shit on a bunch of college students would be a big coup for them."

She was as good as her word. Escorted by campus police, six members of the KKK, including the state grand dragon, filed into the auditorium where my class met. Usually it was only about a third full. Today it was packed to the brim. Five of the six were very large men, prominently tatooed, and not friendly looking. The sixth was trim, neatly dressed, his belly didn't hang over his belt, and he wore extremely dark glasses. You couldn't see his eyes at all, but his mouth was grim and he had a deep short scar along one cheek. Following a twenty-five minute pitch by the grand dragon, he did all of the talking when the grand dragon handed the mike to him to respond to students' questions and comments.

Nearly all the students had their hands up. Their reactions were informed, pointed, nasty, withering. None of it fazed the Klan. The five sitting never blinked an eye at anything the students said. When the essentially masked spokesman didn't want to answer a question directly, he just slid off of it. No amount of redirection could force him, or any of them, to deal with anything they didn't want to deal with. They got their message across repeatedly: "God made different kinds of homo sapiens. One of these kinds just wants the right to be their white selves; to enjoy the company of their natural white peers and not be mongrelized."

"Who do you think is responsible for this mongrelization?" a white student asked sarcastically.

"Not genuine white people," came the reply, as the microphone switched hands.

"I guess you know who's genuine and who's not?"

"Its pretty obvious."

"Why would you think nonwhites are more interested in mixing with whites than whites are in mixing with nonwhites?" demanded a black student.

"Figure it out. You're asking the right question."

"In other words, you're saying white people are the victims in our society, not the other way around?" An Hispanic student challenged with bitter irony.

"That's the way we see it."

"What about slavery? Whites certainly weren't the victims then?" noted an Asian student.

"We're interested in America today. Look at what's happening. Look at your inner cities. Look at your youth on drugs."

"You didn't answer the question. What about slavery?" A white and a black student shouted simultaneously.

"There are all kinds of slavery. What about young kids enslaved by welfare?"

"What do you mean 'enslaved by welfare'?" A young social work student was outraged.

"Decent kids can't get a good education because the money goes to welfare. That's enslavement too."

"That's total bullshit!"

"You've been brainwashed. Open your eyes. Look what goes on around you. Mixing the races doesn't solve their problems or yours. The colored races need their own land, their own culture."

"Dr. Weiner, they're not answering any of our questions!" a dozen voices exclaimed.

The next period we discussed how difficult it is to pin down people with messages. Politicians are masters at changing the subject when they don't want to address an issue. A group of students worked up a plan. They proposed that key questions be mapped out ahead of time. The class would batter a presenter with different variations of a key question until the presenter answered or was clearly exposed as not intending to answer. In this case everyone would sit and stare or boo or walk out. There were other suggestions, which I outlawed.

The group never got the opportunity to try out their strategy. Our next guests, the Black Panthers, were completely forthcoming. They answered all questions directly and made no effort to obfuscate or evade. They had more support within the class than the Klan did, but many students thought they were too extreme, and said so. The one student still wearing boots and a cowboy hat who did not drop the course, a tall, lanky, slow talking boy, was clearly impressed by the Panthers. The fact that they didn't hate stereotypical Uncle Toms confused him, however.

"They kissed our white asses. How can you stand that?" he asked. "They didn't kiss your asses. They thought you were crazy and dangerous. You had all the power. They told you what you wanted to hear. Privately, they hated your guts." His respondent looked very much like him, except that his skin was almost ebony. "Why didn't they ever stand up to us?" "It would have been suicidal."

"But you stand up to us. You don't take any shit off us."

"Times have changed. We're better organized now. We think if we fight you, we have a chance of winning."

"You mean you wouldn't fight us if you thought it was hopeless?" "No, I probably would."

"And you'd probably get killed." "Right."

"So you have more guts than Uncle Toms."

"Maybe less. Maybe it takes more courage to survive than to die."

Following the Panthers was the John Birch Society. They simply ignored the rules. They lectured for the full hour and left hurriedly. Next were the John Brown Revolutionaries, who were as open as their colleagues the Panthers.

About a week after the last presentation, the student who still wore boots and hat to class called me, a little after dusk. "Mr. Weiner, this is Ray, your student." He described himself.

"I remember you. What's up?"

"Do you think maybe you could put me up for the night? I might have a place to stay, but I'm not sure."

"What's the problem?"

"Well, the reason I'm calling you is because I figure you owe it to me, since it's your fault I got kicked out of my house."

"What happened?"

"You know, all that shit we've been talking about in your class, about blacks and whites and all? Well it's sort of made me start looking at things in a different way, and tonight I asked my old man how come whenever he talks about colored people he always calls 'em niggers, and not black people, since he calls us white people."

He paused. I recalled being waked once by a voice on the telephone that said, simply, "Leave town."

"What happened?" I asked.

"Well, he jumped up from the table. Actually, he knocked it over, and went and got his pistol. He pointed it at me and told me that I was either a nigger lover or his son. If I was a nigger lover I could get out of his house. So I left."

Neither of us said anything for a few seconds. "Does he know where you got your ideas?"

"I told him about our class." "Does he know my name?" "Yeah, he does."

"Do you think he might be planning to come after me?"

"Yeah, I think he might. That was the other reason I called you." Ray must have found a place to stay. He didn't come over. For a week or two, we kept our blinds drawn and didn't go out in the front yard much.

There was one other occasion when someone I thought would drop my class didn't. It was a smaller class than introductory sociology, focusing entirely upon phenomena of social stratification. This student also wore a hat and boots, but he never smirked, put his feet on the chair in front of him, or wore his hat during class. He sat in the back left- corner seat and never smiled. He was a large man. The desk was too small for him. No matter how lively the discussion, no matter how inflammatory my comments, he never reacted or participated. He listened and stared.

The final exam for this course was scheduled late in the day. Gradually the classroom emptied, as students finished and piled their papers on my desk. When only four students renaubed in the room, it suddenly occurred to me that the one who sat in the back left corner might be the last to finish. Sure enough, all of the others finally completed their exams. On some pretext, I engaged the penultimate in conversation, hoping to keep him around until the large student in boots finished. To no avail. The very large student was still bent diligently over his paper when the room was empty—except for the two of us. I busied myself at my desk, not able to read, much less grade, a paper.

Peripherally, I saw him close his blue book. He continued to sit for a moment, looking straight at me. I stood up, determined to accept what was coming erect. Slowly, he heaved himself out of his desk and ambled toward me, his blue eyes staring into mine and never smiling. His hands were gigantic. When he was about two yards from me he drew his right arm back without slowing his pace. The arm came forward fast. The hand was open and extended. "Dr. Weiner, I just want to tell you that this is the best damned course I ever had! I still disagree with a lot of things you said, but you damn well made me think!" He shook my hand hard, and left.

I thought about the vice principal at Melanie's school. He would be rolling on the floor. I thought about Melanie, who didn't need to be paranoid in order to look out for herself, and about Hillary, who wasn't the mere product of her background. I thought about the woman who only pretended to mind visiting the homes of black students, so that her peers wouldn't despise her. I had not forgotten Jack's reminder that the themes I dealt with were issues of survival for many people, not just intellectual exercises for ivory tower academicians. But Jack also believed that human survival ultimately means rejecting pathological ways of looking at things, and that people have the capacity—if not the willingness—to do this. I wondered if his pessimism might be more optimistic than my optimism.

Civil Engineering

One of the courses I taught was a graduate seminar on nonquantitative research methods. Students had to define their own research projects. One group wanted to find out if social mores concerning race had changed much in our region. They decided to replicate earlier studies examining whether race affects renting an apartment. Based on these studies, they hypothesized that black couples would still have a harder time than white couples, but a relatively easier time than in the past. They also hypothesized that black-black couples would have an easier time renting than black-white couples, especially if the male was black and the female white. None of their hypotheses were confirmed. White-white couples were vastly preferred and everyone else ran last, about equally. The main thing they learned was that reading about discrimination does not prepare one for the reality of it.

"They were so warm to us and so cold to Brett and Karen!" Arielle, the neatly dressed student who reminded me of Hillary and had brought the Ku Klux Klan, the Black Panthers, the John Birch Society and the John Brown Revolutionaries to address my introductory class was outraged.

"It wasn't their hostility that got to me, so much as their bald- faced lying!" said Karen.

"But can you prove they were lying?" asked Beth.

"One of the procedures we used was for Arielle and Mike to phone and if the manager said they had vacancies, they made an appointment for as soon as possible. Five minutes later, Brett and I phoned and made an appointment immediately after theirs. When Arielle and Mike·showed up the manager would bend over backwards to rent to them. As soon as we saw them leave, Brett and I walked in and suddenly there weren't any vacant apartments. We'd remind the manager that we'd just called less than an hour ago and there were plenty of apartments. He'd look us straight in the face, sincere as you please, and tell us that the vacant apartments had all sprung a gas leak, or all the tenants who were moving decided not to move after all, or a big company suddenly rented all the apartments. We'd asked when this happened. And he'd just lie without even looking the slightest bit guilty. He'd look us right in the eye and say, 'Right after you called.'"

"Can you prove they didn't just dislike you personally?" asked Pete, playing devil's advocate just as seminarians were supposed to do. The object of this course was mainly to refine methodological techniques rather than to acquire information. "Isn't it possible race had nothing to do with it?"

"We tried to neutralize personality effects as much as we could." Mike was ready for this challenge. "For one thing, we all dressed the same way— conservatively. Second, we mixed up the way we coupled, in case we interact with each other differently according to who we're with. Third, after the first few interviews, we started waiting until the very last minute to decide who the couples would be and who would go first. Hopefully, this neutralized overanticipating. The landlords acted the same no matter what we did. When we were all white they were cool. When we weren't, they were assholes."

Pete, Warren and Beth wanted to study the way people react to others who behave deviantly. They hypothesized that very bizarre behavior would generally receive a less negative response than only moderately bizarre behavior, the reason being that the former produced more shock than anger. They tested this hypothesis by sauntering through several restaurants talking loudly and bumping into people; and through several others randomly taking food off of people's plates. They used forks they brought with them. Their hypothesis was only partially confirmed. "A lot of people just thought we were funny no matter what we did."

"Do you really think this is research?" Brett asked.

"Definitely." Warren asserted. He cited the work of a sociologist currently receiving a lot of attention for his effort to create a more scientific, meaning measurable, theory of social control. He recommended collecting as many examples as possible of people's reactions to deviant behavior, and scaling these in various ways. Warren and Beth passed around the researcher's seminal articles and we discussed them the following session. None of them included mention of how many investigators had gotten beaten up while collecting their data.

Two students, Joshua and Arturo, were studying to be civil engineers. Their professor suggested that they might want to combine his class project with mine, if I didn't object. I didn't at all. It was an interesting project. One of the city's main freeways ran alongside the university. The city wanted to expand the freeway. The state was involved because the freeway was part of a state highway. Since some privately held land would be appropriated for the expansion, hearings must be held and decisions made concerning fair compensation, etc. The engineering professor felt this would be a great opportunity for Joshua and Arturo to learn something about the social and political side of civil engineering.

During the next few weeks, as students shared the progress they were making on their various projects and received feedback and criticism, we learned a lot about the bureaucratic processes involved in getting a freeway expansion approved. No one in the seminar found this nearly as interesting as what was happening in the other projects, until the engineering students began to describe how the appropriation of private property was going to be handled. Then everybody became very interested.

On one side of the freeway was a huge parking lot belonging to a retail conglomerate; on the other side, people's homes. These homes were not slums and they were not mansions. They were middle-class and lower middle-class homes belonging mainly to black people. They were among the better homes in the part of town that the freeway crossed at the point of the intended expansion. The plan, apparently, was to condemn only a portion of the property occupied by each of the affected homes and pay the owners accordingly.

"Are you saying that they aren't going to condemn the whole houses? Only part of the front yards?" Beth was stunned.

"That seems to the plan," Joshua affirmed. He didn't seem all that upset by what he was revealing.

"So people will get maybe 30 percent of what their lot is worth, exclusive of improvements?" Mike couldn't believe this.

"Right," said Arturo, who also did not appear to be outraged by his discoveries.

"And the freeway will pass almost directly over their houses?" Warren was beyond incredulous.

"Seems like it," Joshua agreed.

"But that's outrageous! They can't do that!" Karen and Brett exclaimed in unison.

"Well, they're going to have a hearing, and if people in the community think there's a problem, they can come and speak up," Joshua explained.

"When is the hearing?" asked Pete.

"Where is it?" asked Arielle quietly, emphasizing the "where." Joshua and Arturo said they would find out.

Within fifteen minutes after the class ended, the chairman of my department sent for me. He told me that one of the university's senior administrators had asked me to come to meet with him that afternoon. He didn't know why, and I didn't have a clue. I thought about my first summons from the principal of Hillary's school, and decided not to assume that I was going to be complimented for being a wonderful teacher.

It seemed at first that I was completely wrong. The high-ranking administrator put his arm around my shoulder and complimented me on my innovative way of teaching sociology. He told me how he laughed at occasional complaints from parents concerning some of the things my classes discussed. This wasn't high school, after all; this was university. We sat across from one another on an el-shaped sofa. At the other end of his huge office was his huge desk. I thought he might offer me coffee, but he didn't.

Only one small thing concerned him: my methods seminar. He felt that it might have gotten a little off track. It had become a little too unconventional. This was a graduate course, after all, and it might be best to prepare the students to do mainstream sociological research before allowing them to become involved in fringe issues.

I told him that I appreciated his interest in me and wondered how he knew exactly what we were doing in my seminar.

Ignoring my question, he put his arm around my shoulder and told me again how much he valued my contribution. "You have a great future here. Just get that seminar on track!" gently ushering me out of his office.

At the next meeting of the seminar, I told the students about my chat with the high-ranking administrator. Since I had taken immediate recall notes, I was able to play it back for them almost verbatim.

"What does it mean?" Brett asked.

"It means we're in deep shit," Pete answered. "But why? What have we done?" asked Karen.

"Obviously we're stepping on someone's toes." Beth turned to the engineering students. "When and where are they holding that hearing?"

Where, was in the state capital, a city several hours away. When, was the following day, at a midday hour when virtually all of the people affected would normally be at work.

"When was this meeting announced?" asked Warren. "Two days ago," Arturo responded.

"See what I mean? Someone wants this to go through without any hassle," Beth asserted.

"But it's not fair. Those people are going to get screwed!" Mike was almost shouting.

"That's their problem," said Joshua. "They can go to the hearing and protest."

"I don't think so. I think it's our problem. I think we have to get involved." Karen was as angry as Mike.

"This is a research course. We're supposed to be objective investigators," Pete pointed out, not looking at Mike and Karen.

"What if you were investigating murder and saw someone about to get murdered? Would you just watch and take notes?" asked Brett.

Before Pete could respond, Arielle, who had not participated in the discussion thus far, said that she had some further information she had been reluctant to share but now felt she had to. "I found out something this week. I have a friend who works at the planning commission. He says there's been a lot of apartment building lately down in — —." She named a small town thirty miles away. "This town was dying. The highway expansion will open it up. It will come back to life. A lot of people working here will be able to live down there and commute."

"So what? What does that prove?" asked Pete.

"My friend says that some very heavyweight people started buying land down there a couple of years ago," she responded.

Everyone became quiet. Arielle asked, matter of factly, "Dr. Weiner, what do you think we should do?"

I was amazed by how much she reminded me of both Hillary and Melanie. In fact, the seminar reminded me a lot of Melanie's class. Knowledge, for most of these people, was not values on a scale; nor a merely intellectual experience. I said I'd think about it. The bell rang, and within minutes I was summoned to the office of the friendly high- ranking administrator who liked my innovative teaching methods.

This time we didn't sit on the el-shaped sofa. The high-ranking administrator sat behind his huge desk, and I stood. He didn't mince words. "Your job is to teach research methods, not organize political activism." I told him that I wasn't trying to organize activists, but that if academic freedom meant what I understood it to mean, it meant that students had the right to do with knowledge what they would. I thought of the quiet guy and the fifteen year old revolutionary who wanted knowledge to get honkys off their backs; of Melanie, who wanted knowledge no matter what the consequences; of Hillary who wanted knowledge to increase justice in the world. The high-ranking administrator told me that if I persisted I would be fired.

Again I reported to the seminar exactly what occurred. I told them that I thought they should do what they wanted to do, but with full awareness of what they were getting into and what might happen. We explored these possibilities at length during the next few classes.

Some of the students in the seminar—and others who became involved through them—wrote articles to the campus newspaper and to the city newspapers. Others organized people on campus and in the affected community. Some did nothing. At the end of the year I received an award for being one of the best six teachers in the university, and notification that I was fired.

Expulsion

Allegedly, my expulsion was for having too few publications, even though I had more publications than junior faculty members who received promotions. I demanded a hearing. Officials of the university treated me like a minor annoyance. They ignored student protests on my behalf. On the other hand, the most prestigious member of the law faculty was invited to chair my hearing. An assistant attorney general was brought in from the state capital to present the university's case. No errant assistant professor had ever received such attention. I made the newspapers and television.

Sociology students organized other students. They organized people in the community. A famous folk singer sang part of a benefit concert on my behalf. The students put their analytical training to work. They wrote eloquent articles, petitioned officials with impeccable arguments, and studied social change strategies.

One group studied the exploits of early labor organizers in America. They were especially intrigued by a radical syndicalist organization called the Wobblies, who liked to blow things up. The students baked a cake for a sociology department party to which students were invited. It was in honor of a faculty member whose identification with student concerns was transparently hypocritical. He should have conferred with his friend the youth expert. Since he didn't, he accepted the students' gift as appropriate homage. Fortunately, the cake was saturated with a laxative rather than high explosives.

The students were easily identified. Threatened with expulsion and possibly jail, they were frightened. I was accused of inciting them. Everyone began to understand that political activism was different than analyzing society and formulating brilliant hypotheses. Actually testing sociological hypotheses could be as dangerous as fooling around with dynamite. One had to anticipate the consequences.

Things turned nastier still. Big men leaned on my car in the parking lot, casually moving off only when I was a couple of feet from them. They stood just inside the entrance to the auditorium when my introductory sociology classes met. Our phone line made funny clicking sounds. We were awakened by late-night callers who breathed heavily.

The high-level administrator who had threatened me, broke university precedent and rules to address the committee that selected annual best teaching award recipients. He urged the committee not to consider me. The committee consisted of students, faculty, and alumni. Students wrote brilliant, wonderful letters, not just in support of me, but also upholding high academic standards, institutional honesty, and fair play—and they were individually intimidated. Faculty who supported me were threatened. An assistant professor of English with many publications was fired for the outrageous reason that his publications were not consistent with the academic direction his department was likely to take in the future. They hated Jack, who supported and assisted me openly, more passionately than ever, but couldn't touch him because he had tenure. Alumni were petitioned. None of it did any good. I got the award anyway. And I was fired anyway.

When it was all over, I couldn't make myself feel depressed. I wasn't even as anxious as usual about being out of work. Shula was amused. She said I had gone through a rite of passage. She was right. Until then, I had not experienced sustained exposure to personal threat. Jack regarded me like a captain whose West Point lieutenant had come through his first battle respectably. Shula, who ran messages for the Haganah as a child and ducked bullets in a foxhole during the Sinai campaign, smiled approvingly. I was actually proud.

For many students it was the beginning of their real involvement in a society that had seemed merely insane. Now they perceived the purposes and the machinery of power. If these were terrible and awesome, they were no longer mysteries. Only mysterious things seem truly indomitable. Moreover, these students had demonstrated to themselves, no less than to others, how worthy of respect they were. Never again would they allow a self-serving institution to define them.

Like Melanie and her classmates, they also learned that the cause of degeneracy is almost always economic greed. Had my graduate seminar involved only ordinary controversial issues, such as race, sex, religion, or politics, the university would not have fired me, and the state attorney general certainly would not have sent a member of his staff to prosecute me. Unfortunately, the seminar brought to light high-powered investments and profits. Real sociology is not what sociology professors are supposed to teach.

Part Six

The "Real" World

Training and Recruiting

When I found myself between jobs, my grandmother came through. She had a friend in the city where we lived whose son was a prominent businessman. He had a friend who offered to hire me to do a specific job. If I was successful, my position with his company could become permanent. My assignment was to improve collections at the company's local division, which was also its largest branch. Apparently, the sales force was more interested in selling products then making certain the company got paid for them. Since commissions were based on sales figures, this was not surprising. Before me, a large consulting firm had been hired to analyze why collections were so pitiful and charged a substantial fee to come to exactly this conclusion.

Following the consulting firm's advice, the company offered both carrot and stick incentives to the salespeople to do a better job. It didn't work. They fired some, and hired new people who were indoctrinated from the beginning to focus on collecting. This didn't work either. Hiring me was not exactly a last-ditch effort, rather an afterthought. Management didn't expect me to be successful. They were simply doing my grandmother a favor. I perceived that this was an impossible job, likely to last two or three months; but I took it nevertheless.

I made appointments with the various salespeople, who, at this point in the company's history were all men, to accompany them on their rounds. They were not overly happy about this, initially, but got used to it. They didn't have a choice. From my point of view it was not an unpleasant task. The salesmen were nice guys and very interesting to talk to. Moreover, they were good at their jobs. It was a pleasure to watch them in action. They treated me amiably, but didn't take me seriously—until one day when I actually did the job I was getting paid for.

The salesman I was with—Lenny, a skinny, self-effacing man who insinuated himself inside customers' defenses so subtly they were never aware when their attitude toward him changed from polite tolerance to active involvement—called mainly on purchasing agents employed by giant corporations. Late one Friday afternoon we were calling on one of his most lucrative accounts, which was also one of the corporation's slowest paying customers.

Lenny was actually in danger of losing this account. He instructed me to pretend to be a person from corporate management. Maybe the customer would realize that the matter of payment was serious business. He had tried this approach before using the branch's sales manager, but it didn't work. He figured that as long as I was along anyway, it was worth another try. We approached the purchasing agent, a stout bald man named Marty, ensconced in a windowless cubicle papered with posters of essentially nude women. Marty sincerely regretted that our company hadn't been paid yet. "I sent those invoices in two months ago. You need to get after those accounts payable assholes"! "I did that last time," Lenny replied patiently, "and the time before that, and the time before that. I've done it at least ten times. They say they don't get the invoices."

"Bullshit! They've got their heads totally up their ass. Keep after them. You'll get paid." Marty leaned back in his chair, feet on his desk, and casually addressed this advice to me, who had not uttered a word, rather than to Lenny.

Before he could remonstrate, I grabbed Lenny's arm and stated that we would go to accounts payable. We had to find our way through a labyrinthine system of offices to get there, but eventually we found ourselves sitting at a desk occupied by the manager of that department, a thin man with a moustache. He listened patiently to Lenny, who tried hard to impress upon him that the situation had become really critical, indicating the significance of my presence. The accounts payable manager glanced at me without expression and disappeared into the labyrinth. Ten minutes later he returned and informed us that accounts payable had never received the invoices. He asked Lenny for the numbers of the invoices and said he would follow up.

Lenny glared at me, less with disgust than resignation. My presence had impressed no one. He shrugged and shook his head. "Shit! I'm going to lose the goddamn account!"

I suggested we have a cup of coffee and try to figure out what was going on.

"Hell, we know what's going on. Accounts payable is screwing up." He was angry and deflated.

"Maybe not," I countered.

He stared at me, not quite daring to hope there was another possibility—one he could cope with.

"There are two possibilities," I observed. "One, accounts payable is screwing up. Two, Marty is screwing you around."

"Marty? Why should he? He likes me. I send him a case of scotch every Christmas."

"Why would accounts payable screw you, in particular?"

He thought about it. The answer hit him between the eyes. "Because the goddamned CEO says so! He tells accounts payable when to pay. And there's no way I can get to him or prove he's responsible."

"I seriously doubt he actually tells them which bills not to pay you," I responded.

Lenny sipped his coffee and pondered this riddle.

"What you're saying is, the CEO doesn't tell anybody He just makes it happen?" He was starting to think sociologically. "He pressures accounts payables who pressures Marty. Marty is always saying there's no way he can do his job on the budget they give him. So he sits on invoices." Lenny was better than a lot of my students who liked watching me reason through problems but hated doing it themselves. Maybe because he had more incentive.

We paid our bill and retraced our steps to the purchasing agent's office. "Listen, Marty," Lenny forewent small talk. "No more bullshit. I realize they don't give you enough money to pay all your invoices. So you sit on a few for sixty or ninety days. What I want to know is, why always fucking mine?"

Marty didn't say a word or change expression. He and Lenny stared at each other for a while. A lot of nonverbal communication was going on.

"OK, two things," Lenny said at last. "Because I love you and appreciate your business, I'm sending you a case of scotch, and its not even Christmas. Second, if you don't pay my goddamned invoices I'm going to lose this account. Am I right?" turning to me. I nodded.

Marty smiled, shook Lenny's hand, and we left. The account started paying on time. Lenny received accolades from corporate headquarters. The word spread that I might be useful after all.

The salesmen were sharp. They quickly grasped the concept that CEOs don't actually tell department managers not to pay accounts on time. They simply design things so that some bills won't get paid on time. The salesmen knew that management always covers its ass. Getting paid was a matter of figuring out how, in each separate case, a customer's accounts payable system was ingeniously designed to fail so that no manager could be blamed.

At one company, accounts payable were handled by twenty or thirty young women. They filled a large room. Each processed a number of accounts, which changed more or less randomly according to complicated invoice numbering criteria. Many were high school dropouts, most were basically unqualified for the job they were hired to do, and all were minimally trained. These employees were bound to screw up accounts—often. The way for a salesman to get paid was to find out which accounts payable clerk was responsible for his account—any given month—and then stay attentively in touch with her. Liquor was rarely required, but candy helped a lot.

Once again, I was involved in real sociology. The students in the seminar that had gotten me fired would have loved this stuff. At another corporation, neither the accounts payable department nor the purchasing agent was responsible for paying invoices. But no one explained this to Dave, the salesman, a big burly good-natured guy, and a good student. One day he asked his customer, "You know, Sam, how I've been coming to you for months to get paid and you always tell me to be patient? Let me ask you a question, Sam. Do you actually have the authority to pay my invoices?"

Sam remembered some paperwork he needed to finish. Bent over in his shirtsleeves, only the bald spot on his head visible to us standing over him, he took about three minutes reading and signing documents and deciding whether to tell the Dave the truth. "Actually, no," he finally admitted without looking up.

"Who does?"

"I can't tell you that."

"What the hell do you mean, you can't tell me, Sam? Come on, tell me who pays me, for Christ's sake!" Dave's voice expressed joviality humor but his eyes were unamused.

Sam tried to look at him, but couldn't. "Marketing."

"Marketing? What the hell does marketing have to do with our business?"

"I don't know. That's the system. Marketing."

We took the elevator up three flights, to an obscure part of the store which Dave had never visited, containing a sort of storage warehouse and, way at the back, some offices. A small sign on the receptionist's desk said Marketing. Within minutes we were sitting across the desk from a vice president of this division, who immediately acknowledged that they handled the payment of our account. He also admitted that accounts such as ours were handled by accounts payable or purchasing in perhaps every other establishment in the entire world. No explanation was offered concerning the reason for his institution's departure from the norm. He warmly apologized for payment delays, explaining that the company was updating its accounting systems. "Occasionally glitches occur. We're sorry."

It didn't take brilliance to realize that this updating process had begun in the ancient past and would be completed somewhere around eternity. The salesman's invoices had to go from purchasing to accounts payable to marketing. Every step along the way was fraught with hazards. "Do you have any objection if I help troubleshoot some of these, uh, glitches?" Dave asked, reading my mind.

"You can try. It may not do much good."

"If you get my invoices faster, will you pay them faster?"

"Our policy is always to pay on time. If we have the invoices." Once again, liquor lubricated the system. Glitches dissolved in it, and Dave's invoices began to flow, unobstructed, from purchasing to accounts payable.

I was so successful at improving collections that I received a bonus and a promotion. I became an assistant sales manager. Unfortunately, as the salesmen become better sociologists, I had less to do. I continued to ride around with them, and took Shula for an expensive lunch once a week on my expense account. The salesmen advised me that it would actually be bad for the company if I didn't use my expense account. It was tax-deductible. If Shula and I didn't eat expensive lunches, the company would have to pay higher taxes.

The salesmen also told me one of the basic facts of life in industry: If one finds one's claim to fame petering out, as was happening to me, one had better find something new to do—or else learn how to hide effectively. They doubted that I could do the latter. It required a kind of sophistication I lacked. I wanted to take this as a compliment, but Shula pointed out, cryptically, sounding exactly like Jack and the vice principal of Melanie's school: "You don't know what it means to be a pawn."

She was right, I had to acknowledge grudgingly. My deficiency resulted not so much from strong character as from the failure fully to realize what it means to be a powerless person. Many of the salesmen had clawed their way out of a stratum that punishes people who try to be other than mediocre. In this stratum, one of the sociological skills people acquire is how to pretend to be ordinary. The vice principal had had to submerge his dynamic qualities for twenty years. I had never operated with less than a hundred percent of whatever enthusiasm I felt. I had never held back.

Luckily, I didn't have to. I had noticed that the company spent a lot of money recruiting and training salesmen for the division that employed me. They paid a consulting firm to screen and evaluate every applicant. Then each new recruit spent six months learning the operation of every department in the division, before calling on a single account. Late one afternoon, I knocked on the division manager's door and boldly volunteered to take over recruiting, and to redesign training so that it would take only a few weeks to get salesmen out on the street and productive.

"He's crazy!" stated the sales manager who was immediately summoned.

"Let's give him a chance," the division manager, a large bald man with an angelic smile and cold eyes offered benevolently. The sales manager and I sat on opposite ends of a long leather couch across the room from the division manager, who stayed seated behind his desk. The sales manager, a big man with a mane of dark wavy hair glared at me as I tried to make eye contact with the division manager to express appreciation. But he was looking at the sales manager. The division manager now had a kind of hungry, unpleasant expression on his face. I had already been told that he was not fond of the sales manager. Several years before, the sales manager had tried to stab the division manager in the back to promote the interests of a department head who wanted the division manager's job—someone who would presumably turn a blind eye to some of the sales manager's less than kosher practices, which every salesman in the division knew about. The division manager had everything to gain and nothing to lose by giving me a shot. If I succeeded, he would take credit and probably offer me the sales manager's job. If I failed, he'd get rid of corporate dead wood—me. My grandmother's friend's son's friend's hands would be clean, and the division manager would be in his debt.

The sales manager assumed that I had no experience at personnel recruiting and training. He wasn't worried, he told the salesmen. One serious screwup and I was finished. He, on the other hand, would still be around—laughing, and getting even with people who had befriended me.

I possessed, however, if not an ace, a least a Jack in the hole. Not all of my previous life had been spent teaching in secondary schools and universities. I had grown up in a family business. My parents were always complaining about how long it took to train young women to do bookkeeping tasks, which were complicated in our business. "As soon as they learn, they leave and get married!" my mother complained over and over. She was the one who had to train them, and it drove her crazy.

One especially frustrating summer, preceding my senior year in high school, I told her they were going about things all wrong. I said they should stop looking for girls with high school degrees and of good moral character, and just look for girls who were good at things related to the job. My mother stopped what she was doing and listened to me. Then she called my father over and he listened. But that was all the response I got until about a year later, after two hiring disasters in quick succession. They said, "OK, Big Mouth. You do it!"

I ran an ad and began interviewing applicants. I ignored prior references. I was unconcerned with whether applicants had made good grades or had even graduated from high school. I devised my own testing systems to determine whether people were smart in the ways the job required. It had always taken my parents nearly half a year to train young women possessed of high school diplomas and good grades to do bookkeeping tasks. I hired girls with bad grades and no diplomas, and had them competent within a month.

On the other hand, I had a tendency to fall in love with my trainees. This destabilized the office even more than my mother's constant grumbling. Finally my parents laid down the law: they insisted I hire people I wasn't attracted to. I did, and those employees stayed with our company even after my parents sold it to a conglomerate—until the employees reached retirement age.

The company that now employed me also looked for the wrong kinds of attributes in the salesmen they hired. Like my parents, they wanted all employees, including salesmen, to have good moral character and a high grade-point average. However, the most productive salesmen working for the company were unstable, sometimes degenerate, and had been poor students. I learned that they had been hired before the company became so wealthy that it could engage a consulting firm to refine recruitment and training and design a training program which the local division manager admitted he had always felt to be an overlong process. Since many of the new recruits were unsuccessful, it was also very costly. In his opinion, only a very little knowledge of most of his division's systems had anything to do with sales.

I set up a simple interview procedure. I received applicants in a tiny office, little more than a cubicle. It contained a desk, two chairs, and a couple of wall posters. First, I would ask if they knew more or less what our company did. They usually had at least a vague idea. Then I instructed them, "Given only what you already know, and assuming that all you know about me, your customer, is what you can perceive from this office we're meeting in, what would you try to sell me, and how would you go about it?"

The applicants invariably fell into two groups, regardless of how much they already knew about the company's business: members of the first group broke out in cold sweats and went dumb; members of the second came up with some ideas. The latter qualified as serious candidates, and I rejected the former out of hand, regardless of any other qualifications.

I recruited people who could do what needed to be done, and taught them only what they needed to know. They were on the streets and productive in less than a month, and were earning their draw within a three months. As a bonus, the company allowed me to recruit their first saleswomen, and their first black and brown salespeople. All were successful—in spite of the sales manager's diligent efforts to thwart them and me. The local division manager decided not to fire the sales manager. It was more strategic, and more gratifying, to keep him around on a tight leash.

I felt that the work I was doing was not so different than what I had been doing as a teacher, except that more was at stake. If I made theoretical mistakes in this setting my students would suffer in very non-theoretical ways—and so would I. For the first time I thought I understood what Jack, and perhaps students I had accused of wearing rose colored glasses had been trying to tell me: it is easy to analyze issues intellectually if nothing personal is at stake. For most people, most of the time, a lot personal is at stake. I told Shula that maybe no one should be allowed to teach other people anything until they had to risk their position or their salary on the competence of their thinking. She agreed, but assured me that I had already done that.

Hatchet Work

The company that rewarded me by allowing me to recruit women, also gave me a substantial promotion. This included a new office at corporate headquarters and a clearly defined job. I was to travel around to the company's various branch operations and help them improve their recruiting and training procedures. I set off with no misgivings. Alarms didn't go off when the manager of my first assignment—a self-made athletic man in his forties—stated right off the bat, without a smile, that he had nothing to hide and welcomed my audit. I told him I wasn't an auditor. I was there to help, if he could use my services. "You're my boss. Tell me what you want me to do."

He ignored my self-job-description and continued to treat me like an examiner. He unsmilingly showed me his whole operation, including his books. He introduced me to his staff and invited me to speak with them privately. He told them, in my presence, that anything they said to me would not be held against them. I believed him.

Since my opinion of his overall management skills seemed to be the only thing that was important to him, I tried to evaluate these. Mostly, this was beyond my expertise, which I indicated to him. I felt that he believed me, however, he behaved, I felt, bewildered, as though this fact was irrelevant. On the last day of my visit I told him that he seemed to me competent, honest, and frugal. We sat his office, over cokes and potato chips. He sat back in his chair and stared at a tiny black spot on the ceiling. Without moving, he said that having gotten to know me he believed I was honest and sincere. This didn't, however, seem to make him any happier about my visit than when I had first arrived. After a while I left him still staring at the ceiling, and went home.

I returned to headquarters and told the CEO, the friend of my grandmother's friend's son, that the branch I had visited didn't seem to need any help recruiting and training people. He was a relatively young man who had inherited his position from his father. He had just come off the golf course and was still slightly sweating through a light sweater. As though he hadn't heard what I said, he leaned toward me and asked with raised eyebrows, "How is that sonofabitch doing? Is he fucking up as bad as I think he is?"

I repeated that as far as I could tell, the manager in question seemed to be doing a great job. I could definitely say that he handled personnel well, but about the rest of it—marketing, costing, manufacturing—I could only make educated guesses. The young CEO pulled a cigar from a leather box on his desk, sat back in his chair with it unlit and assessed me in a not unfriendly, amused way. He concentrated on lighting the cigar, and then told me what my next assignment was. Over a period of several months I was to visit all of the company's out- of-town branches, each in a different city or town. I would help them with training and recruitment tasks, but also keep an eye out for any management practices that seemed noteworthy.

The first few visits went pretty much as the first one had. Occasionally, I made a couple of suggestions concerning recruitment and training. Even then, my reports to corporate headquarters were positive. So far as I could tell, the company's managers were good. Like the older salesmen I had worked with earlier, the branch managers had been hired during tough times, when the present CEO was still in high school and the company was still clawing its way to the top. Not one of them was actually friendly to me, but all were formally, and humorlessly, completely cooperative.

On about my fifth visit, the branch manager, a man who had been with the company for more than a quarter of a century, treated me with a reserve that went beyond formality. He greeted me briefly, turned me over to an assistant, and didn't speak to me again until I was walking out the door and leaving town. He said goodbye without offering to shake hands. When I returned to corporate headquarters, before reporting to the CEO, I called the local division manager—the person who had given me first my big break and settled a vendetta in the process. Over lunch, I described what I had been doing for the past couple of months, and with what consequences. I asked him if he had any idea what was going on.

Without preamble, He told me that I was being used as a hatchet man. The reports I was turning in were going in the wastebasket.

"You mean they're saying I dumped on those people?"

"To put it mildly. I wouldn't advise you to go out of town without an armed escort," he smiled kindly, but not because he was making a joke. He was completely serious.

"But why?"

"You're the sociologist. Figure it out."

He dug into his chicken-fried steak with relish, while I only stared at mine. "The company doesn't need aggressive, competent managers anymore? Being well-established, they can get by with mediocre bureaucrats? It's all a matter of reducing costs?" I asked at last. "That's part of the story, but not the main part. This is still a family company. Kids are growing up. They need jobs."

On my next out-of-town assignment, I told the branch manager what was going on, and that he should protect himself. Back at headquarters, I delivered my oral report to the CEO, as usual. Signaling me not to leave, he picked up the phone and dialed the chairman of the board, his cousin. He described my report on the branch manager. His version was different from mine. According to him, I had said that the branch manager was a major liability to the company and should be eased out as soon as possible. Then he told me bluntly, "That sonofabitch called me two hours after you talked to him. You're fired."

This time my grandmother couldn't help me. It turned out she didn't need to. Before I could draw a single unemployment check, I received an offer from the local subsidiary of a national corporation. The company had just received a large contract that would require hiring and training a lot of new personnel. They needed to expand the training department quickly. I told the vice president who interviewed me about my previous job experience. I did not gloss over how I had started out doing training work and ended up being expected to do hatchet work, nor did I fail to mention that this sort of thing was altogether unacceptable to me. He said that this job would only involve training.

At the end of my first week, an experienced coworker took me to a meeting of the professional association that members of our corporate specialty belonged to. "You can make good contacts here," he assured me. One of these new contacts was a corporate trainer with twenty years of experience, mostly with Fortune 500 companies. She informed me that hatchet work was hard to escape in our profession.

"Since we work with all departments, we know what everybody does. Whether we like it or not, we make good spies."

"Its like the Mafia," a colleague added. "Management doesn't trust you until you're covered with so much shit no one else will have you."

"You're perfect for this job," a large red-faced man joined the conversation. "You have a degree in psychology," he added, misunderstanding what somebody had told him. "If a psychologist trashes someone, it seems more professional. Management really likes to have their ass covered that way."

I figured there was no point in mentioning that my degree was in sociology. In terms of the logic of his argument, it wouldn't make much difference. Silently I told myself how glad I was not to be part of their world. I was merely a trainer.

Several months later, I was introduced to a new boss. He had been imported from another city to head up a brand new department created for our subsidiary. This department absorbed the training department, along with two others. My previous manager, a warm, thoroughly competent woman, became my coworker. Our new boss was a thin, hard-looking man who grinned a lot, went to church regularly and was active in youth organizations. He and my coworker who was formerly head of the training department began to have long meetings, from which she emerged looking tense and harrowed. Two weeks later she left the company, presumably to accept a better offer. A week later, my new boss took me off my training assignment and instructed me to focus my attention on the local plant manager. I was to evaluate his handling of personnel, especially concerning how effectively he was implementing our training programs. I hoped that my immediate sense of alarm was only residual paranoia.

Two weeks later I handed my report to the hard thin man. It said that the manager was doing fine. My boss merely glanced at it and handed it back to me, grinning as usual. "That's not satisfactory," he said.

"You want a negative report," I stated rather than asked. "You said it, I didn't," the grin never wavered.

I nodded and left his office, feeling the humorless grin boring into my back. From my cubicle I phoned the secretary of the vice president who had hired me and made an appointment. She called me back just before closing time and told me where to meet him, in half an hour.

We took a secluded booth. He cautioned me not to say anything until we had our drinks and the waitress was busy at other tables. "I know. I know. I said you wouldn't do hatchet work. The situation has changed. The contract fell through."

"So you're getting rid of people?"

"Right. A lot of people. We're changing our whole operation." "Why not just lay them off? Why make them look bad?" "Somebody fucked up and has to cover his ass." He was referring to our division president, who had a reputation for brashness, ruthlessness, and occasional stupidity. He had brought in the grinner, a corporate assassin. The vice president hated him. I told him that I couldn't go along with this new situation.

"You don't have to worry," he said. "Your job is secure. But you have to be on the team. If you can't do that, you'll be out," he told me.

We made eye contact. I hoped I read him correctly. "If I expose this guy, will you write me a good recommendation after they fire me?" I asked.

"You bet!" he answered immediately.

We got drunk, and he told me a story about a genius from academia who had been destroyed by corporate politics. "This guy was an Ivy Leaguer. He had a big reputation in marketing theory. One of our big shots grabs this guy at a cocktail party and dares him to put his money where his mouth is. First thing you know, the professor quits his college job and signs on. They assigned him to headquarters. You know him," he stated the man's name. I did know him. He was one of the subsidiary's vice presidents. A soft-spoken, intelligent, unhappy man.

"Anyhow, he did a fantastic job. Part of the reason was because he had this terrific secretary. She didn't bust her ass because she was in love with him. This girl was ambitious. So he went to the CEO and tried to get her a raise. The CEO said his administrative secretary, the highest- paid secretary in the company, was due to retire soon, and our guy's girl could have her job. He didn't like this, obviously, but what could he do? He told his girl, and she was happy. In less than a year they put together . . . " He named a marketing campaign that generated large profits for the company and was still talked about.

"That was his project?" I asked.

"It was his. He and his secretary worked eighty, sometimes ninety, hour weeks for about six months. About six weeks after they finished the project, the CEO's secretary resigned. Two weeks later he hired somebody from outside. Didn't say a word to our friend about it. He stormed into the CEO's office. The CEO told him he'd changed his mind. Just like that. He wouldn't even give his girl a raise either. Not even a bonus.

"Well, She started raising hell all over the company. The CEO called our guy in and told him to fire her. He told the CEO to fire her himself. The CEO told him that if he didn't do it, he was out. He swore he wouldn't do it. Said he'd go back to the Ivy League at half his salary. But then he thought about it. Talked it over with his wife. He'd lose the project. He had a beautiful home. His wife was always dressed to kill. She and his kids liked their lifestyle. To make a long story short, he fired his girl. Within six months he was an alcoholic."

I wondered about my drinking partner. What had being a corporate vice president done to him? I began to spread the word about who my new boss was and what he was doing. Two months later he called me in and handed me an envelope without a single word, only the grin. I opened it. It was a sizable severance check. Double what I expected. Somebody was at least a little worried. I took it and left.

Shula and I had already decided to leave the city and the country. Our daughters were seven and ten. We had visited Israel twice with them. Israel was like my hometown had been when I was growing up. People didn't have to lock everything, they walked anywhere, anytime, and kids in junior high school didn't use drugs. We were packing our bags when a friend called—one of the contacts I had made in the professional association of workers that management uses as spies and hatchet people, and occasionally as trainers. Someone had approached him about a job, but he was well set. He had heard I was out of work and had already told them about me. I told him I wasn't interested; we were going to Israel. He asked me to interview with them anyway, since he had recommended me. The corporation had an even more impressive name than the one that had just fired me.

The first thing I noticed about the man interviewing me was how massive and ruddy looking he was—

like a rugby player. He sat behind a huge desk facing the doorway, and I sat facing him. He had a round, pleasant face. The way he described the job made it sound innocent and fun. It would involve some job performance evaluating and then some recruiting and training. I would evaluate some sales managers and salespeople, mostly men, and then do some recruiting and training. He said that my friend had told him I was pretty good at this.

I asked him if he would mind if I clarified exactly what the job would entail. I had nothing to lose and was bursting with pent-up rage at people who did what he did. I replayed his job description back to him, however reading between the lines and sugar-coating nothing. I was pretty sure he wasn't quick enough to reach across his wide desk and hit or strangle me before I was out the door and on the street. "In short, these sales managers and their salesmen put your company on the map. They risked a lot and worked extremely long hours. Now that they've done their job, you don't want to pay them the high commissions they earn. But you also don't want to honestly tell them this. You just want to get rid of them, using any dirty trick necessary." My hands were on the edge of the desk, my feet under me for a quick jump start. "You will pay me to do any sleazy thing required to discredit them and run them off, no matter how cowardly, no matter how chickenshit."

He didn't go redder in the face, he didn't even tense up. He lit a cigar, leaned back and smiled. He shoved a piece of paper across the desk at me with a figure written on it. It was twice the highest salary I had ever been paid.

Two days later my friend called me. "You really impressed that guy. He can't understand why you turned him down. He wants me to talk you into it." The company had upped their offer to three times my previous highest salary.

Part Seven

The Middle East

Russians

Israeli friends told me that I would not be prepared for Israel. I told them that this was nonsense. After all, I was a sociologist and I was married to an Israeli. Basically Israelis were Westerners, I perceived. They argued a lot more. But the arguing and other cultural habits were only superficially significant. Non-sociologists—people unable to separate the forest from the trees—assigned such things a lot more relevance than they deserved.

The first inkling that Israelis might actually not be particularly Western came at 7:30 A.M. on a weekday when I was driving alone into the city from Shula's parents' home on the outskirts of Tel Aviv. I found myself in stalled traffic, just as I would have in any large city in the United States at that time of the morning. The people in the cars around me looked just like Americans stuck in traffic jams on their way to work look—resigned and bored. The road began to curve, and I could see that there were at least fifty vehicles ahead, and probably more behind me. But in front of the first vehicle was nothing but open road. I stared again and now perceived that the first vehicle was not a car, but a wagon drawn by a donkey. The whole line of cars was proceeding at the wagon's snail's pace, and continued to do so for the next twenty minutes, until it finally turned right onto a dirt road cut through fields of sunflowers. Then we car drivers all sped up.

I was confused. Israeli drivers are assertive. They honk if you are a split second late responding to a green light or even look like you are going to cut in front of them. But nobody had honked at the rude wagon driver. Clearly he was an asshole. There was a wide shoulder beside the road. He could have pulled over until the line of traffic passed. In fact, he could have driven on the shoulder all the way to his cutoff. When I reached my destination, I told the people I was meeting with about this incident. They all said exactly the same thing: "He has the same right to the road that you have."

"But what about the rights of the many versus the rights of the one?" I implored them. The only answer I received was shrugs. In the United States mine would have been a powerful argument. In the Middle East it was meaningless.

The second inkling came one afternoon in Jerusalem. I came upon a crowd surrounding four or five men who were shouting, gesturing, and straining at one another, while ten or twelve others held them back. A woman carrying grocery bags told me what was going on. Two donkey carts had collided with each other at the intersection, even though the streets were wide. The carts weren't speeding. No one was injured. I could see that the carts weren't damaged. I asked which of the protagonists were the donkey drivers. She pointed across the street, beyond the crowd. All I could see was an orange juice stand. I asked her again.

"There, in the kiosk!" she said impatiently.

"Do you mean those two guys drinking juice together?" "Yes, yes," keeping her eyes on the combatants.

"Then who are those people?" I asked.

"They are still arguing about who had the right of way."

The third inkling came one day when Shula and I were having a discussion while walking along one of the main streets of Tel Aviv. My mother called our discussions arguments, but she never lived in the Middle East. In the Middle East, an argument is when people are ready to come to blows, which is much rarer than in the United States. Even then, people usually don't start shouting at one another unless there are other people around to hold them back. As our discussion became more intense, a stranger began to walk closely behind us, listening to our conversation. I accelerated our pace. He kept up. Then he was joining in. Shula turned to him, and began speaking in Hebrew too fast for me to understand. He responded. We all stopped. I assumed she was giving him hell for bothering us. They went back and forth. After about five minutes he left, and we continued on our way. I asked Shula what they had talked about for so long. Was he so crazy he just wouldn't get the message and leave us alone?

It turned out that Shula had not been admonishing the intruder at all. She had been explaining the details of our disagreement to him. He had presented some pretty good arguments, it turned out—in my favor, actually. I was astounded. "I can't believe you just automatically shared our private business with a complete stranger," I complained.

"I never thought about it that way," she answered, and I could see that she really meant it.

Israelis regard one another as members of the same family. Sometimes they hate one another, but they are never strangers. The Russian immigrants understood this and used it to good advantage. Unlike me, who waited politely in lines, accepted being put off by bureaucrats, and got treated impatiently by everyone, the Russians rudely demanded what they wanted and got it. I always felt I was disliked because many Americans really were rich and crass, as they were accused of being, even though I wasn't either one. I felt guilty about being of a rich and crass ilk, and accepted hostility as my due. The Russians understood that already settled Israelis disliked all immigrants for one reason or another. No one deserved this hostility. The rationale for disliking Russian immigrants was that they demanded too much. The Russians answered that they had suffered the longest time in the diaspora and deserved special treatment. They fought fire with fire, irrationality with irrationality. Unlike me, they knew that they were members of the family and had to be accepted. When I finally learned how to be more rudely demanding, I received better treatment at the hands of bureaucrats, waiters, and clerks. People actually liked me better.

Sometimes being considered rich and crass had its advantages. No matter how individual Israelis might feel, the Israeli government liked well-educated immigrants who brought money. The government generally treated Western immigrants better than they did Eastern immigrants. For example, I was not called into the army until I had already been in the country for two years.

Everyone in Israel is a soldier. Every single man woman, and child. The country will never be conquered because everyone will fight to the death rather than give up. Every new immigrant is required to undergo military training. That I had received basic training from the United States infantry and was now in my forties were irrelevant facts. The particular group I reported to duty with were mostly Russians around my age. This was not unusual because of the large number of Russian immigrants to Israel during the seventies. Most of them had also received army training already, more intensive than mine. They were tough, cynical, excellent shots, and knew how to fight. They didn't mind army routine in Israel. It was luxurious compared to what they had experienced in the Russian army.

What they did mind was having to put up with injustice in their new homeland. They considered it unfair that they were called to duty within a few months of their having arrived in Israel. They weren't settled yet. They didn't have jobs and they didn't know Hebrew. I had received free Hebrew instruction for several months when we first arrived, and was already fairly fluent by the time I went in the army. I already had a job. The straw that broke the camel's back was the Russians' discovery that they couldn't even receive an advance on their first month's army pay so their families could eat. The army wouldn't debate the matter. It had its routines. The matter was closed.

It was still an open issue for the Russians, however. They came from a country where people knew how to organize and how to play chess. The first thing the Russian soldiers did was stop shaving and making their beds. The Israeli sergeants threatened to court-martial the Russian soldiers. They said, "Go ahead. Make fools of yourselves." The lower-grade officers wanted to throw the Russians immediately into the stockade, just as Russian officers would have done. The base commander knew that he would have to answer to still higher ranking superiors for causing the spotlight of public opinion to shine upon them. He couldn't ignore the fact that the Russians were, after all, Jews, and therefore family members. The Israeli press would be most unsympathetic to a base commander who threw uncooperative Russian soldiers who were also uprooted, unpaid, and un-Hebrewed in jail for failing to shave.

The next thing the Russians did was follow orders to the letter. One night I was on guard duty outside my barracks. A shot rang out. I darted inside the barracks and was nearly trampled by everyone inside rushing to see what was going on. Two barracks away, a sergeant was lying on the ground, pleading with a Russian soldier to accept his surrender. The soldier pointed his rifle at him until an officer came to take charge. The soldier explained that the sergeant had come too near to the place he was guarding. According to orders, the soldier had challenged him for the password. The sergeant had said something like "Yeah, OK, you're doing a good job," and continued on his way. The soldier did what he had been told to do next: he challenged the sergeant again, and when he got no response, he fired over the sergeant's head. The second challenge and the shot came less than a hundredth of a second apart. The bullet passed about a sixteenth of an inch over the sergeant's head. He could feel his hair part. The sergeant, on still shaking legs, told the officer that the soldier knew him very well.

"I train that asshole every day!"

Everyone was by now gathered close around the shaken sergeant, the trigger-happy young soldier in training, and the officer who was trying to sort things out. One of the trainee's countrymen pointed out that we had all been instructed to require the correct password from anyone entering our area. "No conditions were mentioned. We were not told to forget about the password if a person is an officer, or the base commander, or even the prime minister," the thin, bearded man with a scar on his back, where a superior in the Russian army had struck him with a bridle bit years ago, stated emphatically in bad Hebrew with a thick Russian accent.

The officer glared at him. "The army would never give an order like that!" However, even if an enemy was trying to infiltrate our training post—a possibility so unlikely that it was ridiculous—how did the guard explain the fact that the enemy looked exactly like his sergeant? "You are expected to use common sense!" the officer shouted.

The officer decided to court-martial the Russian guard for not using common sense. The Russian soldiers, en masse, marched to the officers' compound and submitted a written petition. It said that since the army was very strict about some things, like not paying people, they assumed it was strict about everything. If the army wanted to court-martial them for not shaving, they were welcome to do so. But they couldn't court-martial them for following orders.

The matter was dropped. Our training continued, and every-thing was more or less peaceful—like a volcano before it erupts. A week later, Russian soldiers followed orders again. Two squads from our unit that consisted entirely of Russians—Russian recruits made up about 80 percent of our training unit—were guarding adjacent areas. One squad got lost and wandered outside the perimeter of the base. Before long, the other squad saw dark shadows—clearly human silhouettes—fluttering in the darkness. When challenged, the shadows didn't know the password. The challenging squad opened fire. The shadows responded. The two groups fired furiously at one another, doing no damage, until authorities arrived to sort things out. The causers of the melee, the "shadows," claimed they had misunderstood where they were supposed to be on guard because of their poor Hebrew. It was one of their major complaints that, unlike Israeli immigrants from other parts of the world, Russians were taken into the army before they knew Hebrew. It was clearly the army's fault that they had not understood the password. Nobody got court-martialed this time either.

The third time orders were strictly obeyed occurred the following week, also during guard duty. It happened during the changing of the guard. The sleepy sergeant of the guard took the finishing-up guard squads through their mandatory weapons-clearing drill. He forgot one step and gave us the order to pull the trigger on our empty rifle chambers before they were empty. We all cleared the chambers and then pulled the trigger—except for the Russian soldier standing nearest to the sergeant. His bullet went straight into the ground an inch from the sergeant's foot, and the sergeant of the guard went straight up into the air.

They sent my entire unit home several weeks earlier than our tour of duty was scheduled to run. I learned a lot from the Russians, who had been persecuted for being Jews both by tsarists and Bolsheviks. Becoming organized can help, if those in power feel morally obligated to live up to certain principles. I wondered how this might apply to Melanie and third-period class. Did their country feel a moral obligation to regard them as citizens, as it claimed it did? Israel felt no moral obligation to regard Arabs as citizens. It interpreted their organizing as a dangerous act, to be dealt with harshly. The organized Russian recruits I trained with were able to put pressure on the Israeli establishment. If they had tried the same tactics in their former homeland, they would have been killed. Why, I wondered, do governments feel morally obligated to some people and not to others? The face of the vice principal of Melanie's school popped into my consciousness. His expression was indulgent. It said: "Morality has nothing to do with it."

Bedouins

My first introduction to Bedouins occurred when Shula and I became members of a brand new environmental education project based at a research and development community in the Negev Desert. The project's first goal was to design an innovative approach to secondary education. This involved moulding a standard high school curriculum around a core curriculum in ecology. The children of the scientists and engineers working and living in the community were to be our guinea pigs, as students of a new experimental high school still under construction. Until its completion they continued to attend schools in nearby kibbutzim. The new curriculum would include many field trips. Physicists, chemists, biologists and ecologists helped design the project. Science and secondary education interacted to a degree heretofore only dreamed about in Israel, and most other places.

The second, and most important goal of the project was to conduct groundbreaking seminars for educators from Israel, and all over the world on how to do environmental education. It was an ambitious project, taken seriously by Israeli educators and scientists and by ecologists from major universities in the United States, Europe and India. Toward the end of our second year, an international mini- conference on ecology and environmental education held in our tiny community was well attended — to our relief and delight.

The first group of teachers recruited by the project joined project leaders and scientists as members of the administrative team. I was one of the teachers, and Shula was the project director's administrative assistant. Her bilingual skills and no-nonsense efficiencywere invaluable. For us teachers to be valuable, the project leaders felt it essential that we deeply perceive our immediate environment, the Negev. Another way in which Israelis were not Western, I discovered, was that they did not feel obligated to sharply separate the analytical from the poetic. Our leaders wanted us not merely to know about the desert; they wanted us to feel it.

Therefore, twice a week our little group arose before dawn and experienced the Negev. Our community was situated on one border of the Wilderness of

Zinn, where Moses and his wild bunch supposedly wandered for forty years until they managed to break into the Fertile Crescent. Zinn is stark and beautiful. The desert is rich with wildlife and unusual rock formations. Our trainers were people specialized in ecology. Some were geologists, some were biologists, many had no degrees. All were good hikers. We walked long distances, summer and winter. In winter it was bitterly cold in the desert, but none of us complained. What we were doing made sense. Our trainers were low- key. They let us soak up what was obvious. They didn't lecture or pontificate.

Toward the end of our training, we were taken to visit Bedouins. They lived in tents in the desert and raised goats for food and trade. Their tents were large and comfortable. The desert floor inside the tents was covered by beautiful rugs. They offered us coffee and tea spiced with cardamom. Our trainers talked to us about our Bedouin hosts, even as they served us. Our trainers told us how Bedouins were still ignorant and primitive, sometimes caused problems with their wandering herds, but generally presented no real threat to security. They talked to us about how adept Bedouins were at tracking and surviving in the desert, as though Bedouins were intelligent wolves. Our hosts clearly understood what was being said. They continued to serve us politely. They conducted us like tourists through their compound. I noticed children watching us with blank, uncurious faces. In this manner we visited several Bedouin settlements, like conquering troops surveying our domain.

During our next project meeting, I asked our trainers why we had visited the Bedouin camps. They explained that it was because the Bedouins were a desert people and knew things we needed to know. A brilliant teacher of mathematics asked the question I would have asked next: Why had the trainers, who were so sensitive to nature and so sensitive in teaching us, behaved with utter insensitively toward our Bedouin hosts? The trainers—all young men and women—were Sabras, meaning they had been born in Israel. They said, without emotion, that they didn't know what she was talking about. I sensed that the English teacher—and one or two others—definitely knew what she was talking about. I seconded the math teacher's question, and was tersely informed that we needed to move on to other business. In our project, clearly, environmental sensitivity would embrace only the nonhuman environment.

The next time I met Bedouins was during my army reserve duty one summer. Every year I complained bitterly when I received the two- week call-up. That year, when I griped as usual, Shula was only amused for a day or two. Then her indulgence turned to anger. "I don't want to hear anymore about it," she yelled. "Every year you complain, and every year you have a wonderful time!"

She was right. Every year, without fail, I had a terrific time. From Sabras I learned Israeli poker, a swift, dangerous game for high stakes, played with a short deck. I learned complicated domino strategy from Russians immigrants. From Moroccans I learned to play backgammon with intuition as well as logic.. My Scrabble game   improved immeasurably under the tutelage of a Scrabble expert from England, who never failed to play all his letters at least once and usually two or three times in a game. During the games, my peers told colorful stories about life in their home countries and in Israel.

One summer, one of my duties was to drive around the perimeter of our post in a jeep. One evening, a Bedouin soldier, called a *gashash*—Hebrew for "guide"- silently got in the jeep beside me. He didn't say a word as we drove around the base's long perimeter. As we approached a certain gate, he motioned for me to stop and get out. He took the wheel and drove into the desert, leaving me standing beside the gate. I had been instructed by my sergeant to go along with this unorthodox procedure. I joined the two men at the guard post a few yards away.

They explained to me that there was equipment out in the desert. Sometimes the army paid families of Bedouins to keep an eye on it. The gashash was the go-between. Technically one of us was supposed to go with him, but it was understood that he could go alone if he wanted to— and in fact he had never taken anyone with him. He came back through the gate and picked me up a little before dawn.

The next time the gashash rode with me, I tried to strike up a conversation with him in Hebrew. "English," he said. "Talk to me English." By the time we got to my drop-off point, I understood why he wanted to learn English. He viewed this as his only hope to achieve any kind of social mobility.

Later I met Jewish Israelis from Morocco and Yemen who felt the same way. They were less well organized than the Russians. They were settled in development towns in the desert, rather than in neighborhoods surrounding Tel Aviv where they might hope to find jobs in industry. They felt that they were designated to serve as cheap labor for Israel's dominant group: Jews from Western Europe, or Ashkenazim, who had once been socialists but were now the country's capitalist elite. The Eastern Jews, or Sephardim, could vote at least, and they did. During the time we lived in Israel, they helped to vote the old guard out of power—and suffered bitterly when the new regime did little for them.

The gashash didn't have any illusions about his possibilities of exercising political power. He knew he had to increase his market value. Knowledge of English would help. I began to teach him whenever he had spare time. Some days we got in a couple of hours, other days only twenty minutes.

One night, instead of getting in the jeep beside me, he said, "I drive." When we came to the place where I always disembarked, he didn't stop. We drove about ten miles into the desert.

On top of a hill, an older man and two young men sat around a fire. The gashash joined them. They were all animated, glad to see one another. I gathered he received news of home from them and they received news of the world from him. I sat quietly by the fire. Eventually he introduced me. Everyone shook hands with me, but only the older man made eye contact. Tea was served all around, and they resumed visiting among themselves. After about half an hour, the older man stood up and came and sat by me. We began to talk, half-English, half-Hebrew, a little Spanish. Somehow we communicated.

He had a little formal education and a lot of insight. He understood about people and societies. He said that the Israelis were afraid of the Arabs, afraid they couldn't be trusted.

I said that didn't explain much. No one should understand the irrationality of racism more than Jews.

He said that people have to justify what they do. The Israelis had to believe that Arabs were inadequate or evil in order to exclude them to the extent that the Israelis did.

I said it was the same way in America. People of color were defined as inadequate or evil by people who didn't want to compete with them for jobs.

Also by those in power, he added. The elite often found it convenient to maintain an underclass.

Jews of color in Israel also experienced discrimination, I noted. They are merely defined as inadequate, he noted. We are defined

as evil.

"What about loyalty? What about morality?" I asked.

"Loyalty and morality stop with your immediate family," he said.

"You will die for your wife. You will die for your child. You will not die for your cousin."

We told each other about our lives, and observed how people everywhere behave the same. We drank coffee and watched dawn over the desert. Our conversation stayed with me for days, and years. I think most of it was not even verbal.

Part Eight

Middle America

Deep in the Heart of Texas

We came back from the Middle East to my hometown in the summer of 1983. My father had developed a heart condition that was not physical. Since he also had a physical heart condition, this second heart condition caused serious problems. It caused my mother to tell me that if I didn't return and help him through it, she would probably kill him.

The cause of my father's second heart condition was being fired from the corporation he had sold his business to. The company had kept him on for a number of years, but finally got sick and tired of his perpetual haranguing about service to customers. I tried to explain to him that conglomerates don't have quite the same perspective on customer service, or even profitability, that single-owner businesses do. They tend to operate like the army. They prefer to reduce the cost of doing business. For example, dynamic salespeople require dynamic sales managers to manage them, and these in turn require dynamic vice presidents to manage them. Such personnel are expensive.

"But don't those idiots realize they're losing customers?" my father shouted. Although of Russian Jewish origin, my father looked and behaved like someone from a latin background. He had black wavy hair, dark eyes and was slightly swarthy. He was also six feet tall and used his hands a lot when he expressed excitement, which was usually. His customers loved him but he must have driven his new corporate bosses nuts. My mother, on the other hand, exuded gentle sophistication and class. Sometimes, on first acquaintance, people wondered how she put up with my father. Her skin was milky white, but she had flaming red hair and a temper to match. Ordinarily she had no difficulty keeping my father in line. But this situation was different.

"Think about it." I countered. "How many companies operate the way you did?"

"Nobody anymore," he admitted, gloomily. "All of you sold out to conglomerates."

"They're all the same," he muttered. "None of them give a shit!" "Therefore.. ." I encouraged him to draw the inescapable conclusion.

"Never mind. I get the point." He didn't want to discuss it anymore.

But he never did really get the point. He felt betrayed, lost, useless—broken-hearted. He wallowed in righteous indignation and self-pity. He drove my mother crazy around the house. Then he started hatching crazy schemes.

That's when she called me at work one morning while my father was at the bank giving them hell about an accounting error they had made for the second time. "Everybody accepts this goddamned mediocrity!" he would proclaim. He was a crusader against the degeneration of capitalism at the same time that he believed it to be an ultimately doomed system.

Shula and I were seriously thinking about coming back to the United States anyway. We were becoming uncomfortable with the likelihood that my yearly military service in Israel could cause me to wind up in jail. People in my unit were being assigned to inspect cars and busses carrying Arab Israelis, in case they were carrying weapons or bombs. We fully accepted the fact that security was necessary and that terrorism was a real threat. What we could not accept was using this threat as a justification for harassing and intimidating people and taking pleasure in it. If one did not, one became suspect by one's peers. If one refused to conform, one was arrested. To fit in, one had to become a clone of the person who had once called me in the middle of the night and said, "Leave town."

In short, Israeli fundamentalists found my attitudes as unacceptable as American fundamentalists did. Unfortunately, I was in their midst and under their control in my tiny little corner of military service. In fact, I was in the kind of deep shit Jack knew I had to experience in order to understand. How ironic, I felt, that this should occur in the land of my own people, who had experienced terrible persecution. I wondered what Melanie's class would have made of this.

Shula and I decided that, in any case, immediate pragmatic concerns took precedence over ideological issues. One of our daughters was nearing college age. Most Israeli parents would have loved to send their children to U.S. universities. We could. And, since we found that we wanted very much to be where our children were, we decided to return. People laid guilt trips on us: "How can you leave? How can you do this to us?" Then they admitted that they might very well do the same, given the opportunity.

My hometown had been in the news recently, as one of the most booming places in America. Real estate values were at an all-time high. I applied to all of the high-tech, multinational corporations that had moved in during the last ten years and built facilities on a scale the city had never seen. Several offered me a job if I would relocate. Recruiter- trainers were still working out of regional headquarters, they informed me. Rumors to the contrary, none of the local branches were designated to become regional headquarters. I sensed some sort of handwriting on the wall, but couldn't make out what it said.

Finally, I was hired by the owner of an old-fashioned employment agency. For twenty years he had specialized in placing secretaries and bookkeepers in mostly small family-owned businesses. Suddenly, in what his wife called "a visionary fit," he had signed on a high-tech recruiter he met at a party one night at a wealthy client's home. This dynamic person, who had once held key positions in large corporations, now specialized in helping them steal key people from one another. She was what was known in the industry as a headhunter. She was high-powered and sophisticated.

The small operator's wife, a delicate looking southern lady, was also his hard-working colleague and financial partner. She didn't trust the headhunter, a large framed easterner, for a second. She made this clear to her husband in a steely-eyed manner. Sweating a little, he overrode her objections and set up the headhunter up with an expensive office and a respectable budget. Their business would acquire a whole new dimension, he urged his wife to perceive. He could taste the money and the status that high technology business would bring them. During the weeks that followed, his wife's undiminished misgivings bored through his rose-colored vision. God help him if he turned out to be wrong. He hired me to hedge his bet. I would fully assist my new boss, the head-hunter; but my first loyalty would be to the now-prudent visionary. In other words, I would keep him informed.

The headhunter was indeed high-powered and impressive. I sensed that she knew exactly what I was hired to do but didn't give a damn. The reason quickly became clear. Precisely as the visionary's wife suspected, the headhunter had a goal that did not include enhancing her employers' operation (on her way out the door a few weeks after she was hired, the headhunter expressed full respect for the visionary's wife). The headhunter intended to, and did, accomplish her goal with such speed that by the time the shit hit the fan she was long gone. Her sole interest in the visionary was to use the air-conditioned office he provided, the excellent computer, and the staff, including me—all at no small expense, his wife never ever let him forget—to input a large number of resumes she had somehow acquired before her current job, onto floppies. When I finally figured out that we were not actually going to try to recruit and relocate corporate personnel, that she was going to move on as soon as the resumes she had almost certainly stolen from a previous employer were computerized, I asked her what the deal was. She didn't mind telling me, as she was about finished anyway.

"This town is dead," she explained. "The market isn't here anymore." She named the place the market had already moved to.

"I never heard of it," I stated. "You will, soon."

"How can that be?" I asked. "We're booming. Real estate prices are still going up."

"Take my advice. Don't buy any property. If you have any, sell it now."

"You're putting me on. The *Wall Street Journal* says this is the place to invest."

She looked at me—suddenly feeling very much not the sophisticated sociologist—the way someone who knows the ropes looks at someone who doesn't; the way I may have looked at students, from time to time, although I hoped not. I was too naive to waste time on, on the one hand, but bright enough to be impressed by her acumen, on the other. So she told me.

"Where do you think this prosperity came from? The military. They come in with billions of dollars in contracts, and overnight: boomtown. Lots of jobs, high wages. Hordes of people move in, buy property, consume like crazy. Then all of a sudden the military pulls up stakes and moves out."

I waited while she went to the bathroom, made a phone call, lit a cigarette. I sat glued in front of her desk.

"OK. Why—right? You don't have a clue," she observed. "I'm afraid to express the only reason that comes to mind."

She smiled at me intensely, not a pretty smile. "Hate to admit to yourself how capitalism really works these days? There's no market economy anymore. Supply and demand are puppets. The military pulls all the strings. All they have to do to soften up a labor market is get everybody high on good living and then jerk the carpet out from under 'em. Suddenly shinola turns to shit. Meanwhile, someplace else, shit is turning to shinola. For a while. Then the same thing happens to them. Wait and see. In a few years, the military will come back here with new contracts. People will fight each other for the same jobs they have now, at half the salary."

She told me where she was moving to. About six months later that city was being advertised in the *Wall Street Journal* as the new economic miracle, and the bottom fell out of real estate in mine.

I needed a job again. My mother repeated her suggestion that I return to teaching. I repeated that I could not get a job with the local university.

"Teach high school," she said, taking a drag on a cigarette she couldn't smoke around my father. Since he couldn't manage his business anymore, he managed my mother.

"It doesn't pay worth a damn, and you get no respect," I complained for the umpteenth time.

"It doesn't matter. It's where you belong," she said quietly, leaning toward me, seeing in my eyes that I knew she was right.

This time Shula agreed with her. "It may only be for a year or two anyhow."

They were right. I loved being back in the classroom. My new students were unlike any I had ever taught. They epitomized the American stereotype. With few exceptions, they came from white middle-class families, participated in athletics or the band, went to church on Sundays, and saw absolutely no value in being able to reason. Basically, they were mystics. They considered science to be another belief system. To them, entertaining the hypothesis that the speed of light is a universal constant was not essentially different from believing in the Garden of Eden.

There had been a fair number of anti-intellectuals in Melanie's school as well, but non-rationalism didn't rule. Students assumed that having a powerful mind was an asset. Playing the dozens took a lot of reasoning ability. Students had no difficulty debating issues at length. They could easily sustain a class discussion for two days with no assistance from me. At this school, students could not sustain a class discussion for more than five minutes. At Hillary's school, cynicism had ruled. But it wasn't all that deep. Below the cynicism lurked curiosity. At this school, students seemed to have forgotten how to be curious. In Israel, pragmatism ruled. Students lost patience with theory if it didn't result in a measurable, assessable outcome. But they loved figuring out complicated connections between theory and practice. Logic was a valuable tool and often a weapon. At this school, definitions were an end rather than a means. It didn't occur to students to wonder whether definitions were connected to anything. The Bedouin children I met thirsted for knowledge at every level. Incessantly they asked why. Understanding was an obsession. At this school, understanding was an unnecessary chore.

My new ninth graders were happy to memorize and regurgitate whatever teachers presented to them, so long as the information could be ingested in bite-size segments. Partly this was because they were accustomed to making good grades this way, like the three at Hillary's school who signed a petition and told me I should take advice from other teachers who converted learning into ritualized memorization. Partly, though, it was because my new students enjoyed memorizing for its own sake. It was a comfortable routine. I could teach them nonsense, and they would memorize it. I could teach them sense and show them why it was sense, and they would ignore the rationale and memorize the facts. I urgently explained to them why I thought reason was important. The students perceived this as some sort of obsession that inhabited me. They understood obsession. It was like possession. They were not unresponsive. They responded the way they would to anyone preaching a gospel. They applauded my devotion.

It took me about six weeks to figure everything out. Fortunately I had help. The physics teacher, whose classroom was across the hall from mine, had been through the same process of discovery that was rapidly dumfounding me. "Don't lower your standards," he laughed when I complained that I couldn't seem to make reasoning-based tests easy enough. "Hang in. They'll come up." I thought about the catatonic summer school classes who woke up to talk about pissed-on toilet seats and highly charged words. In a moment of quiet insanity, I toyed with the idea that trying one of these tactics might be worth getting fired. Instead, however, I redefined the curriculum.

"For the time being, I have decided to define science as the study of anything. Whatever you're curious about. I'm not going to present a topic today. You're going to give me one," I told first-period class.

A whirlpool of silence formed near the ceiling of the classroom, sucking my directive into oblivion. I repeated it and stared at them. Finally someone raised her fourteen-year-old hand. "What do you want us to do?"

"Just tell me something you're curious about."

"I can't think of anything." Twenty-eight pairs of brown and blue eyes stared at me out of blank faces.

"Sure you can. Remember when you were little. You were curious about lots of things. What were some of them?"

A few faces screwed up trying to remember, trying to please me. Most remained expressionless. I waited and waited.

"Mr. Weiner, we can't think of anything. Tell us what you want us to do!" A petite girl with a huge orange velvet bow in her dark hair was becoming irritated.

"I already told you. Tell me something you want to know about." "Anything?" A red haired, freckled boy who brought his skateboard to class asked. "Anything," I said. "Really anything?" "Anything!" I repeated.

He glanced around at his peers. His face turned red. "How long is the average penis?" defiantly, not quite suppressing a giggle.

There was a collective gasp. Then, cautious grins, furtive looks at one another. Suddenly curiosity prevailed in the classroom. The whirlpool on the ceiling collapsed. Everyone was saturated with curiosity about what would happen next.

I stared sternly at the class, and at the red haired skater, who stared gamely back. I allowed the silence to become agonizingly pregnant.

"About six inches." I told him, finally, in a pleasant voice, still without smiling. "There have been several fairly scientific surveys about people's sexuality and sexual behavior. Apparently, a lot of men worry about penis length."

The class was stunned. Each student looked at every other to determine if everyone was as stunned as he or she. I realized immediately that it wasn't the question that stunned them, or my answer; it was the fact that I had answered it at all.

After about half a minute of super charged silence, a tall blond girl dressed entirely in black, grinning, checking out her classmates' reactions, asked, "Why are guys so hung up about that?"

From that moment, the class was transformed. They shed embarrassment and silliness and engaged in a pretty fair discussion. Hands were still waving in the air when the bell rang. It was the same in every class, although the topic was sex in only four out of five. Fifth period wanted to talk about prejudice.

I couldn't wait until the next day. Finally there were topics students were curious, even excited, about. We would pursue them in depth. So what if they had nothing to do with the prescribed science curriculum? So what if parents complained? At this point it would be worth it. I beamed at my first-period class while they got seated.

"OK, who wants to start us off today?" Almost immediately a hand went up.

"Why is the sky blue?"

It was the same in every class. Yesterday's hotly debated topics had set with the sun. Dumfounded and deflated, I showed them a videotape about scientific discovery and agonized over what to do next. About midnight I made a decision. I did not share it with Shula, nor did I tell her about my dream where the vice principle of Melanie's school, my friend and mentor, smiled at me grimly, shaking his head from side to side. Next day, I told every class that even though this was a class in natural science, we were going to continue our sociological discussion of the first day's topic that they themselves had brought up, until we had plumbed its depths. "That's what science is all about," I declared. "Using evidence and logic to learn things we don't already know. Not just things you read about in textbooks and science journals. Things you're interested in. Things you care about." I dared to feel encouraged when a tall blond boy raised his hand.

"Mr. Weiner, we've talked enough about that. Let us ask you some more questions."

"Can we go on a field trip?"

"Why don't you do things like Mr. Wizard does? Those are interesting."

I turned my back on the class and stared at the chalkboard behind my desk. Melanie's face appeared. She smiled at me indulgently: "You're going to have to compromise, Mr. Weiner."

She was right, of course. I had to accept the fact that at this school we would not pursue any subject beyond the limits of the fifty- minute class period, and try to make the best of the time available.

"The purpose of science is to understand things," I told them, turning back around. "It really isn't very useful for you just to observe fascinating phenomena and receive short explanations. Its like seeing a motorcycle for the first time and being told the reason it goes is because it has an engine. If you don't know what an engine is, what have you really learned?"

Again silence. Finally, a soccer player spoke for everyone: "But its hard!"

This was the crux of the matter. Like the university freshman, they weren't accustomed to putting two and two together. Asking me questions and getting answers was one thing. Being required to make connections themselves was another.

"Tell me again what you plan to do one of these days to make a living," I asked first period class the next day.

"Go to college," All but one asserted

"What do you want to study?"

"I don't know," the first student on the first row admitted. "What, maybe?"

"Maybe architecture."

"Do you want me to prepare you for college?" I asked the last student on the third row.

"Yeah. For sure." She wanted to be a veterinarian. "How many want me to prepare you for college?"

Only three of my hundred and twenty-five students indicated anything other than a desire to go to college.

"Do you think I know better than you what it takes to get into college? And to make it through?"

Everyone agreed that I probably knew better.

"How many are in sports?" I seemed to change the subject. Nearly everyone's hand went up.

"Do you like to do exercises and run laps?"

Nearly everyone groaned, shaking their heads vigorously. "Why do you do it?"

"Coach says we have to." A first-string basketball player spoke for everyone.

"What if you complained to your coach, like you do to me, and your coach said you don't have to do exercises if you don't want to? Then you could just have fun. Except when you played some other school, of course—then you'd get slaughtered."

"We'd rag out the coach!" Everyone agreed, irritated at the very idea of such a travesty. "So would our parents."

"Why?"

"Because he didn't prepare us!" strongly implying that this was obvious, so why was I asking?

"But you said you didn't want to do exercises."

"A coach isn't supposed to do what you want! He's supposed to make you do what's necessary."

"To win?"

"Of course!" That's what its all about," angry at my continuing to ask stupid questions.

I paced around for a minute or two. "Why don't you see this class the same way?" Suddenly everyone's face went blank, as though someone had cast a spell over the entire class. The whirlpool that absorbed ideas reappeared beneath the ceiling.

"This is different," another athlete finally stated softly in a sullen, irritated tone.

"Really?" Silence.

"Maybe not," an ROTC color guard member finally admitted. In first period, and every period, gradually, grudgingly nearly everyone agreed that it was not at all different—not really, not if people wanted to succeed in life. I perceived that the exercise had not, after all, been a waste of time. For the moment at least, these students acknowledged what Melanie and her classmates had accepted without hesitation: the inevitability of logic.

"From now on look at me the same way you would a coach," I advised as first period came to a close.

"None of our coaches are bald, Mr. Weiner."

Relentlessly I reminded them of this discussion, all through the year— every time they complained that thinking challenges were too taxing and that they would prefer memorization and regurgitation exercises, which they pointed out were the norm in most of their classes. The majority did not learn to love reason, but they grew to accept its legitimacy. What I never succeeded in shaking completely was their belief that some people are born able to reason and others are not. Unfortunately, much of this came from home. One father, angry that mine was the only class in which his daughter made C's, blurted finally: "What do you want from her? She's only a girl!"

Summer School

If regular school students didn't want to do work that required reasoning, my summer school students didn't want to do school work at all. They hated everything about school. The only reason they were in summer school was to make up credits. They had not only failed science, it turned out, but practically everything else as well.

"Why are you failing so many subjects?" I asked them right off the bat. This was an unusual way to begin a course, and they scowled at me for about ten seconds. The answer I received from a thin girl wearing baggy shorts and a white tee shirt emblazoned with a message which was obviously obscene but technically unreadable because of a large rip, seemed to represent the majority of the class's position.

"Because my fucking teacher hated me," she said, glaring defiantly.

I nodded and launched into a brief description of the course, which they already knew, and filled the rest of the two hours—until midmorning recess— with films about penguins, robots, lightening, and a contest at MIT. The contest involved teams of science and engineering students vying to design a machine that could beat opponents' machines at plopping ping pong balls into a hole. The most successful machines employed some strategy for blocking an opponent while plopping in one's own balls. The machine the class liked best—they cheered it loudly—was one that actually destroyed the opponent's machine. The fact that it was too disabled by this accomplishment to plop in its own balls seemed irrelevant to these students.

During the break, I approached the summer school principal and asked if I might be allowed to deal with their alienation before getting into the subject matter of the course. He cautiously agreed, so long as this could be done fairly quickly. I swallowed twice and further requested permission to make an unconventional contract with my students. They seemed to enjoy cursing like sailors. Colorful language was strictly forbidden in the district. Could I allow the students to use colorful language, in my classroom only, if they would go along with my program? He finally agreed to this on the condition that at the first sign of trouble—meaning a complaint from anyone at all—I would cancel the arrangement.

The students loved the idea.

"Hey Mr. Weiner. How come we have to learn fucking science anyway?"

"Don't be fucking stupid. Science rules." "Then how come you fucking failed it?"

They cast side-glances at me to see when I would put a stop to this barrage of profanity.

"Because the goddamned fucking shithead class totally fucking sucked!"

The room went dead silent. It was as though they felt the universe could not fail to react to this way over-the-line affront to normalcy.

"Why did the class suck?" I asked.

It took a half-minute for them to shift gears from expecting Armageddon to talking about something they really wanted to talk about, but probably never had. Since everybody's class had sucked, answers came from everywhere.

"The teacher wouldn't explain anything."

"I hate memorizing a bunch of shit I don't even understand." "We never did anything interesting."

"What would be interesting?" I asked. "Experiments." "Figuring stuff out." "Field trips."

"So you don't really hate science," I observed. "You gotta have science in the modern world." "Science is OK."

"I want to be an engineer."

Everybody wanted to be someone professional, to go to college, to make a lot of money, to be successful. "So why did you fail?" I asked again. During the next hour, everyone confessed.

"Because I'm stupid."

"Because I'm always fucking up." "Because I'm a loser."

Since summer school sessions were four hours long, we didn't have to end a discussion almost as soon as it began. For the next two days we discussed the politics of school. This group was clearly not typical of regular students I taught, and probably not typical of summer school students. On scales of brightness and alienation, they ranked in the top decile on both. They reminded me a lot of third-period class in Melanie's school. They loved analysis and were aware of being on the short end of society's social rewards system, but not for the same reason as Melanie and her classmates. These students were all white. Also unlike Melanie's peers, these summer school students were already convinced that their condition was their own fault. I told them about the boys at Hillary's school whom teachers had defined as mentally unfit– the ones who turned out to be brilliant. I told them about the honor roll girls who petitioned me to stop teaching math as a thinking subject.

I asked them to write an essay on how they thought curricular decisions were made in school. I had given this same assignment to my regular school students the previous year. Most of my regular school students always passed everything and had at least B averages. They had written the briefest of paragraphs and expressed a lot of consternation: "How are we supposed to know this? You haven't covered this!"

Most of the summer school students wrote at least a page, tightly argued and packed with substance. No one thought the assignment unreasonable. Based on what they knew, their analyses were more than competent. I told them so. I also told them how the regular school students had responded. I asked them what they thought it indicated.

"They must not have understood what you wanted." "Maybe you didn't explain it as well as you did to us?"

No one could think of another possibility. I asked them to write a second essay, describing the skills and attitudes people needed to succeed in school. With one exception, they said pretty much what regular school students always said: studying, doing homework, taking notes. The exception, a dark-haired girl dressed in coveralls, named Liz, wrote only one sentence on her paper: "You have to be good at kissing ass."

Liz was fourteen years old, had an angelic face and was built like a linebacker. She had already been suspended for two days of the summer school term when she took exception to the school-bus driver's attitude. During the ride to school, the bus driver thought some kids—not including Liz—were too noisy. According to Liz, he called them "snotty little assholes." Liz invited him to get off the bus and fight her, then and there. When he declined, she told him what she thought of him. Everyone knew that Liz always owned up to her transgressions. She never tried to blame anyone else. The bus driver had probably said what she claimed, the summer school principal agreed. He still had to suspend her, however. Liz had been in an out of foster homes and juvenile detention institutions most of her life. She wrote excellent prose. Her terse response to my question could not be dismissed as mere defiance.

"A couple of days ago you said you fail because you're a loser," I reminded her. "Now you say that to succeed you have to 'kiss ass.' How do these ideas go together?"

"I'm a loser because I don't know how to kiss ass."

"Don't know how or don't want to?" I asked.

"I want to. I just can't."

"So you think it's good to know how to kiss ass?"

"You have to kiss ass," said Linda, who had earned money as a model and during class carved someone's initials into her leg with a pocketknife when I wasn't attentive enough.

"So what about studying, doing homework, all of that?" I asked. "That's all kissing ass," said Chris, whose mother had committed him to a juvenile facility because he had been unmanageable ever since her new boyfriend moved in.

"Do you think that studying is really unnecessary?" I asked.

"No, it is necessary," Liz said. "You can't learn anything if you don't study. But the way they do it, it's kissing ass. I don't know how to explain it."

"Yeah, she's right."

Everybody agreed, but nobody could explain it. "Well what about what we're doing?" I asked. "This isn't school."

"This is a blow-off."

"This is like summer camp."

"You don't feel like you're wasting your summer coming here every day?" I asked.

"No, this is fun!"

"Actually you're doing harder work, more difficult work, than you did in the classes you failed," I told them. "You're good thinkers. You analyze well. You're skeptics. You don't accept something just because it's written in a book or because someone in authority tells you it's so. You want to understand. Understanding is harder than memorizing. The ability to analyze will make you more successful in college and will get you better jobs than the ability to memorize."

My eloquence didn't dent their conventionalism. They didn't believe that what we were doing in summer school had anything to do with schoolwork. We were getting away with murder. For the next two days I guided them through an analysis of how the school as a day care institution, and the school as an educational institution might have somewhat conflicting goals.

"So being a loser is OK?"

"Not a loser, asshole, a non . . ." ". . . Nonconformist."

"Yeah. It's OK to be a nonconformist." "But you still have to kiss ass."

"That doesn't make it right." "Then why do we have to?"

"It's like the army. You have to put up with shit."

"No, you guys still don't get it. What he's saying is that in the real world, what makes us losers in school will make us successful."

"That's crazy!"

The next day I began the class with the announcement that we had to start dealing with the physical science curriculum. "How do you want to approach this? Start with physics or chemistry?"

They didn't want to approach it at all. "So what do you want to do?" I asked.

"I want to play games," Linda stated with a note of defiance. She had allowed me to convince her to stop carving on herself and felt she had a right to demand something in return.

I didn't reply for a moment, and the classroom became quiet. They surmised that I was finally going to do the normal thing: become authoritarian. "Would all of you like that?" I asked.

No response. "Like what?" their expressions asked. "To play games," I elaborated.

Everyone emphatically would.

"OK," I agreed. "You invent the games and we'll play them." "We don't have to do science at all?" Chris asked.

"Nothing is more scientific than inventing a game," I informed him. "To invent a game you have to formulate a hypothesis about what might be fun. Then you have to test your hypothesis, draw conclusions, formulate a new hypothesis if necessary, and then test this hypothesis, until you finally succeed or conclude that your design won't work. Building the game is like designing an experiment." I paused. "There is one condition. The game you invent has to be totally original. It can't be a modification of a game that already exists. This will actually be more difficult than doing the regular curriculum."

This didn't faze anyone. They couldn't wait to begin.

My prediction was accurate. Creating games made the summer school course much more challenging than the course the students had failed. I tried doing the same thing the following year in two of my regular classes, with dismal results. The summer school students did a terrific job. One student created a children's board game which I felt certain was marketable. A group of three organized a paper airplane contest. They operationally defined flight variables and made everyone in the class carefully record data. In addition, everyone had to describe each design modification made on their model and analyze its effect on their plane's flight. Students even looked up articles concerning cutting-edge applications of paper airplane modeling techniques in the aircraft industry.

Another group designed a hilarious obscene board game, modeled on Chutes and Ladders. A fourth group invented a three- dimensional political geography game that could easily be updated based on current events. None of the students ever believed they had done any work during summer school.

Health Class

Health classes were taught mostly by athletic coaches in this school, and the students mainly learned about hygiene. Classes were usually shown a nauseating movie on acne and an even more disgusting one showing what smoking does to a person's lungs. Occasionally there were more health classes than coaches and academic teachers had to teach one or two sections. Being low man on the totem pole, I got one.

Regular class teachers considered health, as an academic subject, to be a joke. It was not prestigious to teach it unless one was a coach. Coaches had more prestige than anyone in the school. Health was simply their small conformity to the intellectual requirements of public education. In fact, the more prestigious the coach, the more likely it was that she or he would only have to teach health and not some other academic subject. When there were more coaches than health classes, however, academic positions were awarded to coaches ahead of people especially well qualified in English, math, science, etc. For regular class teachers, teaching health was a comedown.

The health students I got looked a lot like my nonconformist summer school students, only older. Several of the boys wore earrings, and the girls bragged openly about having affairs. They were juniors and seniors, whereas the summer school students had been freshmen. Like the summer school students, many of the health students had failed frequently. They hadn't dropped out of school, however.

I perceived that I could weight the health curriculum in favor of sociopathology rather than biopathology—precedent notwithstanding. I was new and figured I could assert that I didn't know better, if necessary. Just because the school ignored my sociology degree did not mean that it was right to deprive students of my expertise. I was far and away the most qualified sociology teacher in the school. As a senior elective, sociology was a history department perk allocated on the basis of peer status rather than qualifications, however. In any case, no one cared what anybody taught in a health class. I would be Brer Rabbit thrown into the Briar Patch.

"So why have you failed so many subjects?" I asked them right off the bat, confident after summer school that this would open things up immediately and get us off to a dynamic start.

I received deadpan looks and not a hint of curiosity from anyone in the class. These students were sophisticated.

"Obviously a lot of you are older than most juniors and seniors." I knew I had to shift gears in a hurry. "Also, I've looked at your records."

Often students expressed outrage when I told them this. How dare I? These kids didn't care.

"I thought you might like to get into school politics a little." No response.

"Find out what really determines success in school." No stirrings of any kind.

"You'll be surprised at what you learn. Most people say they blame the system, but really they blame themselves for failure. In fact, there's a lot wrong with the system."

Zero interest. I tried a different tack.

"How many of you are pretty excited about learning health?" No hands.

"How many of you would like to use the time in this class to talk about things you're interested in."

A few hands, finally.

"OK, what would you like to talk about?" No answer after two minutes.

"We can talk about anything you like. No subject is forbidden." No class had ever failed to respond to this offer, if only to test how far they could go. This class didn't.

"Come on! I'm offering you a chance to make this class what you want it to be!"

Still nothing. They were more implacable than the university students who responded only when I told them the story about the pissed-on toilet seats. I was about ready to throw caution entirely to the winds and tell the story again when a long-haired boy raised his hand.

"You're making us a good offer Mr. Weiner, but to be totally honest, I don't really want to talk about anything."

"What do you want?"

"The only thing I want is to feel good now. I don't really want to think about the future."

"Do all of you feel that way?" I asked. All twenty of them did. The bell rang.

Next day, I sat on the corner of my desk and told them that what they had told me at the end of class had occupied a lot of my thinking time since then. I told them I had no idea what to do. "What do you want me to do?" I asked them. "Just check attendance every day and then let you hang out? Or put you under pressure to do something?" This was not a gimmick. I was entirely serious. I had no idea what direction to take.

I fully expected they would prefer the former, and had no idea what I would do in that case. After a while, the long-haired boy surprised me. "You probably ought to put us under some pressure," he said. The entire class agreed with him.

For the next few periods, I nagged, harangued, and pressed them into intellectual inquiry and debate. Gradually, things began to pick up. Discussions started that lasted more than five minutes. I made them take positions on controversial issues, and then change sides. Toward the end of the week, a laid-back boy wearing two different kinds of earings said we really ought to start coming to class stoned. "When you're stoned you have much better discussions," he drawled.

His buddy, both in and outside of the class, confirmed this. "Man, we have profound discussions on weed!"

About half the class smiled and shook their heads. Everybody liked these guys, but nobody took them seriously. I told them to record their next stoned discussion and bring it to class. "But you can't be stoned in class. You have to be straight when we listen to it, and you can't listen to it ahead of time. You have to listen to it for the first time together with all of us."

"Absolutely, man. You'll really be surprised."

They brought a tape a few days later. We listened to fifteen minutes of them babble at one another, neither ever responding to what the other said, pontificating about trivia and nonsense apparently for hours. The whole class, the stoners included, fell out of their chairs laughing. As composure returned, a seventeen year old senior who looked like a twenty-five year old movie star raised her hand. "We need to talk about date rape," she said, still laughing but also serious.

The class grew quiet, but no idea sucking whirlpool hung beneath this ceiling. The quiet was vibrant and intense. First she, and then several young women told about their experiences, and the experiences of females they knew with macho guys who expected something in return for dinner and a movie. When it wasn't offered, they tried to take it, and often succeeded. Usually victims of this kind of abuse did not report such incidents to their parents. Often they blamed themselves as much as the male, but always felt somehow that they didn't deserve blame. All of the girls in the class commented, asked questions, and acknowledged one another's pain and grief.

Those who had been victimized learned what they had not really known for certain before: that they were not alone in having the kinds of feelings they did about what happened to them. They also learned that most of them had never discussed their experience with anyone outside of perhaps one best friend.

During this discussion, the boys sat and listened. Near the end of the period, however, a blond weight lifter who played both varsity football and baseball said that he believed girls brought their victimization upon themselves.

"If you don't want attention, why do you show off your bodies so much?" He asked with a slight smirk. Then he elaborated on how girls dressed, until one girl after another cut him off belligerently, wondering how he equated attention with rape. He didn't mind their hostility.

"What do you expect a guy to do with a three-hour hard-on?" He asked, describing a recent date he had had with a provocatively dressed young women. He leaned back in his desk, one leg propped on the seat of the chair in front of him, arms behind his head, relaxed, confident and defiant. He clearly considered himself to be a proper teenage male role model. Other males could follow his lead or reveal themselves as wimps.

The girls were speechless with fury. The other boys in the class glanced at one another guardedly.

Some wore a sophisticated smile, which might mean anything, but certainly couldn't be seen to indicate disagreement with the jock. Others stared absently into space. One or two became busy with their notebooks.

"What you do with a three-hour hard-on is take it behind a tree," I said at last.

The Jock undraped his leg and stared at me. "You mean masturbate?" He seemed genuinely amazed and affronted. "My religion says masturbating is a sin!" Everyone was wide awake and alert. Sin was not a trivial issue in this school district.

"So you think that God considers violently raping someone to be less sinful?" We stared at each other like two gunfighters. This was a crucial moment, I knew. No one said anything. The atmosphere was intense. Then a quiet girl began to speak. She told about being raped by her mother's boyfriend. Another said her uncle had raped her when she was twelve. Someone knew someone who was having sex with her father and was afraid to tell anyone. The guys in the class— except the jock—began openly to express horror, outrage, disgust, and sadness. The girls could feel their empathy.

"So why did you just sit still when that asshole was putting us down?" a tiny black-haired girl got directly in the face of a husky boy wearing cowboy boots.

He shifted his feet a good deal but found the strength to admit that he didn't agree with people like the jock. He had always been afraid of what other guys would think if he didn't pretend to.

The boy with long hair—the one who had said I should put the class under pressure—now said to the black-haired girl, "I know you think we're all like him, just interested in one thing. Well I'm not. I'm pretty sick of casual sex. I'd really like to have a relationship with somebody." He was a hip musician, popular with the opposite sex.

One after another, the males in the class agreed with what he said. All of them, except the jock, shared the musician's attitude. Each was surprised to discover that the attitude he held secretly was less deviant than the one he stated publicly. They had been afraid to admit that they wanted relationships more than orgasms.

A girl who had bragged about being promiscuous said, "You just don't realize how hard it is. Guys won't pay attention to you if you don't put out."

"Yeah, but girls act like they only want us so they can show off to their girlfriends," a tall boy responded.

That's true," the girl sitting across from him admitted. "We're no better."

The jock moved from the center of the class to a chair on the edge of the spontaneous circle students formed at the beginning of each period we met. For days he read a book or stared out the window. When he now blurted out that he had something to say, everyone was startled. We had forgotten about him. He had become an outsider. The transformation in the class that had brought about his change in status had apparently affected him deeply, however. In a humble, almost pathetic voice, He began to describe his relationship with his mother. Clearly it was not an ordinary mother-son relationship.

"Man, that's way intense," someone observed.

The jock went on to admit that he had always felt insecure around women. He hung his head and we all prayed silently that he was not going to cry. "Sometimes I even think I might be gay," he said at last.

It was hard to empathize with him, though everyone was trying to. The silence was becoming deadly.

"Oh hell," the girl with the rapist uncle finally broke the tension. "Guys are always afraid they're gay. I never understood why you all are so hung up about it."

I took her cue and embarked on a lengthy review of the increasing body of evidence indicating genetic correlates of homosexuality, and the huge amount of testimony by homosexuals indicating that people who are gay or lesbian know that they are from a very early age. "It's not a disease that you can catch." No one followed up on my comments. No one wanted to get deeply involved in the jock's problems. The bell rang. As everyone hurried to leave class, I told them that next period I intended to ask them why they didn't want to talk about the future.

The Future

Most of my students didn't want to think about the future. The health students pretty much summed up everybody's reasons:

"Because there's nothing we can do about it anyway." "Its depressing!"

Melanie and her classmates had looked forward to the future. It was scary, but they still had looked forward to it. Even Hillary's sophisticated classmates had been eager and curious when we talked about the future. How were my present students different? I finally figured it out.

The vast majority of students in this school were white, Anglo Saxon, and Protestant. They all came from the same social-caste level of society—upper—but not from the same socioeconomic level. The higher- class, wealthier white students tended to be in honors, talented and gifted, and advanced placement classes. Other white students, together with most minority students, were in regular classes. I taught regular classes. Unlike Hillary and her classmates, a large percent of these white teenagers were children of members of the dominant stratum of society who had not, according to their own standards, fully realized their birthright. Unlike Melanie and her classmates, or Hillary and her classmates, these young people did not believe that striving would help them much. They saw themselves and their families as dead-end people. Outside of their own church group, they felt they had no status.

There were a few minority students in the school, about half of whom came from wealthy families. All of my minority students wanted to talk about the future. The black kids in particular wanted to figure out who they were and what would become of them. The wealthier black students had a harder time dealing with their black peers from not so wealthy families than they did dealing with white students. The Hispanic students tended to be cynical. They doubted that school would benefit them much, but they intended to better themselves one way or another. Since they had no idea how, discussing the future was of great interest to them. They were careful not to seem too eager about it, however. The Asian American students had no doubts concerning their academic abilities. Many qualified for talented and gifted classes, which had to accept all students with qualifying test scores that were high enough. There was no way to keep them out. On the other hand, there was a movement within the district to eliminate honors, talented and gifted, and advanced placement classes altogether—to mainstream everyone. The Asian American students in my classes wanted to know whether the future offered hope that they would be treated more and more like white people and less and less like black and brown people.

There was one topic involving the future that all of my students were eager to discuss: racism. Discussions about racism revealed exactly how everybody felt about their future prospects. Hispanic students were revolutionaries in their hearts. It was time for a change. They were going to kick ass—somehow. Black students had no intention of letting racism keep them from their goals. Maybe they would work within the system and maybe they wouldn't. Asian American students were angered by racism but not particularly threatened by it. They wanted to know how it operated, so they could figure out how to deal with it. White students said that government preference for minority people was why they, whites, would never get anywhere. No one was more aware of being victims of racism than my white students.

"We're the persecuted ones," a blond-haired boy asserted. "You all can campaign all over school for black rights, but I can't even wear a T-shirt that says White Power."

"Because it's you people who hold us down."

"I don't hold anybody down. I'm not prejudiced." "I bet you're daddy is."

"My father got turned down for a job so they could hire a black guy who wasn't even qualified."

"Maybe, but for a hundred years it was the other way around." "My father had nothing to do with that. All he ever did was try to feed his family."

Practically every hand in the class waved madly. "So you all agree that discrimination is a bad thing?" I asked.

Everybody agreed.

"How many people in this class personally don't like people from other races?"

One of the three black students raised his hand. One of the three Hispanic students raised her hand. None of the twenty-three white students raised their hands. There were no Asian American students in this that class.

"How many have a parent or other relative at home who is seriously prejudiced?"

All the white students raised their hands. One black and one Hispanic hand also went up.

"So most of you do not consider yourselves to be prejudiced." I concluded. "I can believe that from what I see in the halls, from the way you socialize with each other. So why not get rid of racism?"

"We should," agreed a black student.

"It's about time," asserted an Hispanic student.

"It's not possible. It's human nature," stated a white student. "Why is it human nature?"

"People want power over other people."

A feeling of nostalgia swept over me. The presence of Melanie and third-period class were almost tangible. I wished they were truly present to interact with these students.

"This class is part of humanity," I observed. "How many of you would discriminate against other people in order to have power?" I asked them the same question I had asked third period. The white tenth grader whose father had been passed over raised his hand.

"I don't believe you," I said. "You're not like that."
"Well, maybe not. But I wish I was."

"Why?"

"You don't get anywhere if you aren't ruthless."

"That's baloney," a black girl responded. "You don't have to be ruthless."

"We need to change things," a Hispanic boy said.

There was a lull at this point. Nearly everyone considered herself or himself to be unprejudiced yet a victim of prejudice. The real split was between those who felt something could be done about racism and those who thought it was an act of God.

"Maybe it would help to figure out why people are racist," I suggested.

"Yeah. Why do you all hate us?" a Hispanic girl asked. "I don't hate you," a white girl responded.

"Because you know her," another Hispanic girl pointed out. "But some white people are afraid."

"Afraid of what?" a black girl asked. "Anything or anybody that's different."

The whole class agreed that this might be true.

I began the next period by summing up what they had said the day before: "It seems you all agree that racism is a bad thing and you're not in favor of it. You disagree about whether anything can be done about it. In order to figure that out, you need to know why people are racist. Yesterday you all pretty much agreed that it's because of fear. Is that correct?"

Everyone agreed that my summary was accurate.

"Let's test that hypothesis," I proposed. This was, after all, a science class. "Do you believe that if, say, Jeremy"—a black tenth grader who liked everybody—"hated Martin"—a clearly open-minded white tenth grader and one of Jeremy's best friends—"this would be essentially the same thing as Martin hating Jeremy?"

Everyone laughed at the ridiculous scenario of Jeremy and Martin hating one another. They affirmed, however, that both situations would be equally bad and qualitatively the same.

"What about a person with a gun hating a person without a gun, all other things about them being the same? Are these two situations equal?" I asked.

"No way!" James, a red-haired boy stated everyone's opinion. "Why not?" I asked.

"The dude with the gun can shoot the other dude. The dude without the gun can't do anything."

"So you're saying it doesn't matter if someone hates me if he can't hurt me?" a black teenager asked.

"Well, does it?" "Not really."

"Who has power in this country?"

"Whites," asserted all the black and Hispanic students and one or two white students.

"Wait a minute!" Martin said. "You're saying I have more power than Jeremy? That's bull!"

"If you and Jeremy go traveling together, anywhere, not just in the Deep South, who do you think will get hassled and who won't?" I asked.

"But that's totally unfair! I don't want it. I don't want to be treated different than Jeremy—or anybody else."

"That's the point he's trying to make," Jeremy said. "We don't either one of us have a choice."

The boy whose white father had been aced out of a job by a less-qualified black person spoke again. "I don't have any power and never will," he said.

"But in the larger scheme of things, do people of color have as much power as white people in this country? Do they earn as high salaries? Do they get the best jobs? I'm not talking about the few who get better jobs, but the majority. Do you really think that minorities have more economic power than whites?" I asked.

"I think they have more than we do," he answered.

"So you're not afraid of us because we're different. You're just afraid we might be smarter than you?. We might take your jobs? It's all about money?" a quiet, intelligent girl asked, shocked by what she was learning.

This class was typical of all of my classes. About half of the white students agreed with the white teenager who felt powerless. White dominance in the abstract meant nothing to them. Unless they experienced its effects firsthand, they would not admit that it existed. Eventually about half of them did accept the possibility that nearly everybody was powerless. Maybe the real split in society had nothing to do with skin color or ethnicity. In that case, they felt, nothing could be done about it. No more than a third of my white students believed that political organization could bring about social change. Most of the minority students, on the other hand, felt that it definitely might be worth a shot.

About a third of my white students remained strong in their belief that only a resurgence of white pride would make a difference for them personally. Of all my students, this group's skepticism concerning the value of intellectual achievement was the most profound. More than any of my other students, they perceived no good reason to strive for a good education, academic or vocational competence, greater skill at being rational and logical. I both pitied and feared these young people. They seemed to lack any faith in their own ability to determine their lives. No students I had ever met possessed lower self-esteem. In the absence of hope, they abandoned all idealism. Their adoption of mysticism was a coldly rational strategy. Instinctively, they trusted brute force more than reasoning to accomplish their goals. This was the kind of competition they knew they could win at. They had the numbers, and not much skill would be required.

Afterword

Science, Religion and Race

After fourteen years, on the brink of the new millenium, I have been forced to leave the high school teaching position I loved. I have left other jobs, of course, but this separation is bitterly hard. The grief comes in waves: relief, anger, pain. It reminds me of the same empty hurt I felt when my mother's death set in. Not as intense, nearly, but of the same sort.

Colleagues—friends, dear friends, I acknowledge, and am overwhelmed by the realization—call to express their support. And their fear.

"Could this happen to me?" they wonder aloud.

"I have been doing this or that with my students."

"A few years ago some or another incident occurred." "Could it happen to me?"

My responses are both reassuring and alarming to them. I tell them how much more extreme I have been in my teaching methods than they are. But I also tell them that I don't think that it really matters. It is a question of whether or not they are targeted. If they are targeted, it doesn't matter whether they have been pushing the envelope or not.

My story begins several years ago.

I was teaching a high school course called physical science, which included elements of both chemistry and physics. A student who seemed to especially like me brought me offerings of articles and essays by creationist proponents almost daily. She called these proponents scientists. She frequently raised her hand during class to inform me that my presentation of big bang hypotheses and findings was unfair, since I didn't teach creationist ideas about how things came to be. Polite and patient, her manner seemed almost motherly—like one applying gentle but relentless pressure upon an errant child. She never presented arguments, merely restated her simple position.

At first her classmates supported and admired her for taking the risk of challenging a teacher. But gradually the climate changed. The other students' interest changed to tolerance, then to impatience, and finally to irritation. Some students expressed belligerence, which I quelled, insisting that everyone's questions merited respect.

And I responded to her challenge. I painted the complex canvas of how we have come to define knowledge in Western society. I shaped science and religion as separate but vitally important systems of knowledge. I shaded in the particular richness of each and drew the sharp boundary between them. A new and fascinating subject of the course emerged: The Ways in Which People Know Things.

The only student who failed to derive value from what she had helped to create was my inquisitor. Her manner became hard. She seemed frustrated and unhappy, and the intensity of her attacks increased. She no longer expressed tolerant affection for me. I watched helplessly as she became the tragic victim of a charade she seemed compelled to act out. She could not support her position, even minimally, in argument with her own peers. She could only state absolute truisms. I assumed that she had been sent forth, ill prepared, by powerful figures unknown to me, to do battle in my classroom.

Eventually I learned more about her situation. I was summoned to a meeting with the vice principal—and her parents. The meeting began in a friendly manner. Her parents had brought a sheaf of creationist material that they wished to persuade me to include in my curriculum.

I did not ask them—as I might have done—whether any of their documents included the generation of a single testable hypothesis, such as "it is hypothesized that on, or about, the following date, the following creature will be created." Nor did I point out that big bang and evolution theories generate scads of testable hypotheses. If some don't hold up, it doesn't matter, because science proceeds from wrong guess to wrong guess. It stumbles and fumbles its way along. But without testable hypotheses, even fumbling and stumbling are impossible.

What I said, simply, was that public school teachers are required to teach science as it is, not as they might independently wish to define it. For practical purposes, in our society "science" is what is published in peer review journals, such as *Science, Scientific American,* and *Nature.* I told them that if any of the creationists they wanted me to include in my curriculum were publishing in peer review journals, I would be obligated—and happy—to teach students about them and their work.

Conversation stopped dead for perhaps half a minute. The parents stared at their laps, as though in prayer, but when they looked up their faces were firm with resolve. The mother pulled a small notepad from her purse. Her notes were neatly written, I could see, in blue ink.

"On such and such a date," she read, "you blasphemed in front of the whole class. On such and such a date, you called our daughter 'Little Miss Christian' in front of the entire class. On such and such a date, you told the class that you are an atheist and urged them to become atheists as well." When she had finished, she closed the notepad and returned it to her purse. Both parents sat blank-faced and silent.

I glanced at the vice principal. His jaw had fallen open. Literally. He stared incredulously at the couple, who strenuously ignored us both.

After a pause I stated for the record that none of what the mother had "documented" had, in fact, occurred. The only charge containing even a shred of truth was the "Little Miss Christian" taunt, which had been hurled by a fed-up student. I had told the student that if he or anyone else made such a comment again, they would be sent out of the class with a discipline referral.

After relating this, I asked the parents if they wanted their daughter to be transferred to another class. "That's what we want," the father replied. The vice principal said nothing. There was another long pause. At length, I stated quietly that it was OK with me. And it was done.

The next morning the principal, a fairly new arrival to our school district, met with the vice principal and me. The principal asked us why we had given in so easily. "I would have supported you," he told us.

The vice principal and I shared a brief glance. I explained to the principal that we believed the parents' true intention was not to express concern over their child's education but to send a message—not just to me, but to all the teachers and administrators who would hear about the incident. The heart of this message was that these parents represented a group, one that would use whatever means necessary to accomplish their goals.

On this particular occasion they had told outrageous lies—lies so flagrant that the teacher in question—me—was in no real danger of censure. However, if challenged or crossed, their future lies might be far from harmless. If they had claimed, for instance, that I had sexually molested their child, there would be virtually no way for my administration to protect me.

The principal admitted that I was right. He acknowledged that in some school districts teachers live in perpetual fear of such a charge. And that even when the charge fails to hold up—as is usually the case—the damage to the teacher in question, especially when that teacher is male, is permanent.

During the following months, evidence continued to pile up, confirming that my run-in with the parents who wanted me to teach creationism was part of an ongoing campaign aimed at teachers and administrators throughout the district. At inter-school workshops, teachers I had never met before recounted my experience with the creationist parents, not knowing that I was the teacher in question. They told stories of similar encounters involving other teachers.

I learned that the cumulative effect of these attacks was an epidemic of self-censorship. Biology teachers stopped teaching evolution theory for fear of attack, even though it was still a required part of their curriculum. Physics and chemistry teachers neglected to mention big bang theory, even when discussing the creation of atoms.

Once while we gathered around the coffee urn at a workshop, a new teacher noted some recent victories of what she called rational people over extremists on the public battlefields of textbook adoption, school board elections, and curriculum revision. But the oldtimers only shook their heads cynically. In their opinion, the public simply failed to perceive what was happening. Though the extremists were losing the little public skirmishes, they were winning the larger war as teachers, afraid to do otherwise, revised their curricula—voluntarily—and administrators observed passively.

I did not self-censor. From time to time a student would advise me that I should either stop teaching big bang theory or should teach creationism as well. I always agreed to transfer an unhappy student, and felt lucky that that was all that was demanded of me.

Another facet of my teaching approach that disturbed some students—and parents—was my lack of strict adherence to the school's mandated textbook for my course. All students were required to take this, or a similar course, as part of the required curriculum. Rarely did one of my students indicate an intention to major in physics or engineering or mathematics in college, and most stated that they would not have signed up for this physical science course voluntarily. Aware of these facts, I endeavored to make the course meaningful within the context of their interests and concerns, as well as pertinent to the State- mandated curriculum.

In order to accomplish these goals, I found it necessary to "stretch" the textbook. The first stretch always involved describing to my students how any discipline that attempts to explain the cause-and-effect relationships among any variables endeavors to apply the methodological principals first developed by physicists. Such disciplines include psychology, sociology, political science, and anthropology, in addition to the hard sciences.

I also mentioned that while my bachelor's degree was in a hard science—chemistry—my Ph.D. was in the soft science of sociology. My doctoral minor was in social psychology and, as a graduate student, the sociology of science, religion, and intergroup relations (including race relations) had been of special interest to me. I felt this information was important for students so they would know my qualifications for leading them in directions that might depart somewhat from the conventional physics curriculum.

I then asked students to identify issues they wanted to investigate, whether or not they fell within the scope of hard science. I explained that we would devote a small but substantial amount of time to exploring these topics. Any question would be acceptable as long as it had greater significance than merely the potential to satisfy narrow curiosity, and as long as everyone in class felt comfortable with it.

I gave examples of questions students had asked in the past, such as "What are black holes?" "Are there aliens in space?" "Is time travel possible?" "Are Nostradamus' predictions true?" "Do flying saucers exist?" and, on a different note, "Why is society racist?" "Why did Columbine occur?" as well as "Why do people abuse drugs?" "Why are boys only interested in one thing?" "How can we protect ourselves against AIDs (without giving up sex)?" and "Why are some people homosexual?"

It was allegedly parents' discomfort with my willingness to include such "controversial" topics that caused the administration suddenly to redefine my pedagogical freedom. This was the same administration that had demonstrably accepted my "deviations" for years, that had occasionally chided but never condemned me for being controversial, and that had encouraged parents to meet with me to openly discuss my methods.

On this occasion, I was informed that parents had already been informed that my classroom methods would not be tolerated—before the administration even met with me. I was ordered not to depart from the official curriculum in the future—not even one iota. I was told that this requirement was for my own good as well as the administration's. These things were said in a manner that projected frustration and anger but also desperation. I felt only a deep sadness at the time, and responded that I was not certain that I could do what was required.

The next day I was summoned to a meeting with members of both my school and district administration. The atmosphere was not friendly. They immediately asked why I felt it necessary to depart from the technical hard science curriculum in teaching my classes. I explained that I felt (and shall always feel) committed, both as a professional educator and as an ethical person, to enhancing young people's ability to communicate openly and honestly in a non-confrontational way. This is one of the most valuable and precious skills my students can learn, I asserted.

The extracurricular, sometimes controversial discussions that I held with my students never interfered with their mastery of the textbook material. On the contrary, I believed that these discussions substantially enhanced their mastery of hard science challenges. More than any technique in my repertoire, allowing students to choose to use logic, rather than attempting to force them to use it, seemed to break through their resistance to using it (a resistance that plagues many teachers).

The discussions allowed my students to choose to use logic creatively toward ends they themselves decided were important. They challenged one another's most deeply held ideas and, as a result, thought their own ideas through more fully. This to me had always been what learning was all about. And valuable information came to light. Questions such as "Can some people predict the future?" as well as "Are people of color really inferior to white people?" allowed students, logically and systematically, to discover from each other—and from me— why we come to believe certain things in our society, even when they are not true.

I felt the administrators were hearing me. There was a long pause before one of them stated that they might be willing to go along with some of this but not the discussion of sexual topics. I replied that for many of my students, perhaps most, these classroom discussions were the first time they had communicated certain of their most private thoughts and fears to anyone, whether peer or authority figure. For example, many boys felt pressured by their peers and the culture to pressure girls to have sex with them. It was a relief for many boys to discover that other boys were also feeling this pressure and that they were not alone among their male cohorts in wanting intimacy even more than sex. Since AIDs is perhaps the greatest threat to our young people today, strengthening teenagers' ability to resist pressures to have casual sex would seem to be a rather important educational goal, I concluded.

The administrators all regarded me quietly for a while. I felt I had reached them. The next day I officially received the conditions I must satisfy in order to keep my job. I had to state unequivocally, in writing, that (1) I would stay strictly within the most narrowly defined confines of my curriculum, and (2) I would not to teach in a manner than anyone could consider controversial. I resigned.

I am not certain which puzzles me more: the swiftness, the suddenness, and the harshness with which my fall from grace occurred, or the fact that I was tolerated for as long as I was. One possibility that occurs to me is that, until recently, I was most valuable to my attackers as a working maverick—a sort of convenient, always available target. Every time a student was transferred from one of my classes, other teachers knew about it and became more afraid. However, somehow, I don't feel that this was the reason—or at least not the main reason.

In the end, I believe I was tolerated because I was a good teacher. I strengthened students' ability to deal with issues that, when ignored, often destroy lives and families. In the final analysis, I was, among other things, an effective role model: an advocate and a motivator of ethical behavior, sexual restraint, and resistance to drug abuse. Most parents allowed their children to remain in my class. Some checked me out, from time to time, but did not ask me to stop what I was doing.

On the other hand, perhaps I walked a line that grew thinner and thinner over time—until I finally overstepped it. I know that each year I became increasingly aware of my students' need to be treated as people of value in the present—as people with pressing educational needs that exceeded the school's formal curricula—rather than merely as future candidates for this honor. As I became more competent at reaching my students, did I also become more threatening to the community that paid my salary? Or did something in the community change, causing what I was doing to become more threatening?

During the last two years, one particular change occurred that strikes me as dramatic. The number of students who expressed discomfort when I discussed big bang or evolution theory increased significantly. Before that, an average of one or two per class were unhappy during discussions of these subjects; but in the last two years, in some classes, more than half the students present insisted that science constituted a belief system in competition, and conflict, with their religion.

Like the student whose classmates had all finally became irritated with her, the students who were challenging me now vigorously displayed their position as though it were a banner inscribed with a slogan which they assumed was true, although they seemed to have no idea what it implied. A very small amount of questioning was sufficient to reveal that they did not know enough about science even to make assumptions concerning how it approached issues of knowledge. However, a diminishing number of their fellow students expressed irritation with this authoritative position. Like my earlier student, those loyal to the slogan appeared to have been shallowly indoctrinated by sources invisible to me, sources that somehow commanded everyone's respect, if not allegiance.

Sometimes when I found myself confronted by a group in rebellion against big bang theory I would say to a class, "All right, we won't deal with this subject this year in this class." The dissenting students would invariably insist that I explain how I could subscribe to a belief that was wrong. I would ask them what belief they were referring to. Big-bang theory, they would state. I would reply that I was not aware that any scientific theory could be classified as a belief. I understood scientific theory to be something quite different from religious belief. Then I would attempt to change the subject, and pursue a physics topic not related to big bang theory.

They would not, however, accept their apparent victory in dissuading me from presenting big bang theory. They insisted that I explain how I viewed it, if not as a belief. Their essential curiosity, intelligence and fundamental love of learning were apparently stronger than their indoctrination. I explained that during the last several hundred years in our society, scientific theory and religious belief evolved into entirely separate and different ways of knowing things. The cause-and-effect logic of a scientific theory does not require it to be true in the religious sense, merely testable. For example, Newtonian theory, which physicists consider to be false in its basic premises, is still the tool that everyone uses—scientists and devout believers alike—to create new mechanical devices.

The students affirmed that according to the rules of their religion, as they understood them, the testing of beliefs according to the criteria of science was inappropriate—blasphemous, in fact. They fully agreed, on the other hand, that failure to test a scientific theory would be equally inappropriate—it would be irrational. They almost always concluded, therefore, that the rejection of big bang scientific theory on religious grounds is unsound from the perspective of either logic or belief. Nevertheless, many persisted in holding tightly to this rejection.

When I examined this paradox (which I found startling), my students revealed themselves to be more worldly than I had realized. Some openly stated that their opposition to science on religious grounds was a result of their need to remain solidly connected within their community. Unless one was very very wealthy, they pointed out (often quoting me), one needed a support group in order to make it in the real world.

The support group they referred to was not just any group. The students who rejected science tended to be aggressively Caucasian. In class after class, some students insisted that white people needed all the reinforcement they could get, because white people were presently the most victimized group in American society. Examples were given of fathers, uncles, and older brothers who had been passed over for jobs because they were white.

Oddly, the same students who argued that American employers systematically ignored the intelligence and competence of white people in order to show preference to minorities also tended to be the very same students who insisted that weak academic performance was almost always due to low native intelligence. In other words, if students performed poorly, it was because they were not smart enough to do better. Even more disturbing to me was the fact that these students seemed to make their academic choices—such as their selection of courses to take, of colleges and universities to apply to, and of occupations to strive for in later life—based on their estimation of their own ability. Their estimation was usually much lower than my own.

Most of my white students, however, and nearly all of the minority students I taught seemed to hold themselves in higher esteem—at least as regarded their inherent abilities. Often black or Hispanic students expressed exasperation, even despair, but I would rarely get the impression that they believed they lacked basic potential. In the minds of my minority students, poor performance most often was the result of poor preparation or lack of motivation, not an innate inability to do better.

When I spoke with the parents of low-achieving students about their children's performance in class, I encountered the same sets of assumptions. The parents of most of my white students and most of my minority students often assumed that their kids were not trying hard enough. The parents of white students who thought of science as a religion, however, tended to believe that my high standards might be unrealistic when applied to their children. Implicit in this, I felt, was their conviction that education was not the key to getting their children to where they needed to be in life.

I learned through discussions with colleagues that I was not alone in observing that many of our students' parents failed to assign to education the same value that we teachers did. And that, in addition, intellectual growth as a primary life goal, seemed to be losing ground as a strong value in the community we served. Some members of the community seemed to prefer to instill in students a brand of religious piety that rejects discovery and imagination, offering, in their stead, indoctrination and dogma.

How, I agonized, could caring parents accept these substitutions? How could they allow their children to grow up ignorant in a society that has made such advances in information technology, and whose best employment opportunities require good logic skills? How could they reject sound thinking in favor of non-rational mysticism?

Logic dictated what my next question must be: "Is it possible that an educational philosophy which makes no sense intellectually might nevertheless possess some practical value for the people subscribing to it?" It frightened me to realize there was some evidence that this might be the case.

Support for this hypothesis came to light during a discussion about racism, always a favorite topic among my students. At some point, in almost every class, someone would suggest that different racial and ethnic groups might really differ genetically with respect to basic intelligence, that this would explain why some groups fared better than others in our society. The counter argument, that racial discrimination exists and that not everyone has the same opportunity for social mobility, almost always immediately followed the question of genetic superiority.

This issue almost always led to heated debate, usually with no end in sight. After a while I would interrupt the vocal class argument to ask how we might approach resolving this question. What I wanted my students to observe was that the rational way to resolve important issues was not through passionate verbal conflict, but through logical analysis and systematic research. I offered bonus points to students who would dig up any existing studies pertinent to this question, and said that we would continue the discussion at that time.

What next happened — with increasing frequency over the years — both surprised and disturbed me. Certain of the same students who earlier had insisted that people of color receive preferential treatment over white people in the present-day United States — the same students who argued that learning science conflicted with their religious beliefs — would now state that white people must stick together in order to keep from losing out in the competitive struggle for good jobs. I checked and double-checked to make sure that these students meant what it sounded like they were saying — that they would lose out in competition on an open playing field, where all players had equal opportunity.

My attempts at verification led to the response that this was precisely what was meant. In addition, many of those students who so attested admitted that this viewpoint was also the outlook of their immediate and extended families and friends. This information left me to conclude with sadness and alarm that many of my nonminority students, as well as the significant other people in their lives, apparently believed themselves to be at a disadvantage in our society, not because they lacked political clout or opportunity, but because they lacked the ability to achieve. Perhaps even more disturbing, however, was the perception that, concerning my apparently most religious students, the meaning of belief for them may have become very substantially colored by the perceived need of their community to achieve a pragmatic adult political goal: white solidarity within a fundamentalist framework.

What has changed in this community, I fear, is the degree to which the consideration of the welfare of children has been overwhelmed by other considerations that have also been present all along: considerations of economics, politics, and group solidarity, all packaged together as religious piety. Commitment to both the emotional and intellectual growth of children has been overwhelmed by adoption of the ideology of anti-intellectualism. This ideology rejects all systematic forms of knowledge, and with them the obligation to be systematic at all.

If I am correct, then teachers like me probably can no longer exist in communities like this one. If this community expands, then perhaps there will be no place in our society for teachers like me. I feel no animosity for the people who want to destroy true education. I sense that they do so out of desperation.

I find it difficult to accept that those who advocate fundamentalism really believe that science is evil and that their form of religion has the potential to purify our society. What their children manifest appears to be a fear of forces too strong to negotiate with, much less struggle against. The "little" people of society, including themselves, can only fight over the crumbs left behind by the "bigger" people. The way to be certain of getting the most crumbs for one's own family is not through personal achievement, but through superior group strength.

Religion for them, I feel, has become the focus for organizing such strength. In the process it would seem to lose much of its capacity to nurture young people in ways that enable them to develop a sense of their own strength and beauty.

It seems to me bitterly ironic that if the group that may eventually come to dominate in the struggle to control education is the group that most devalues it, they will nevertheless be the only group in a position to receive any education at all. I feel, however, that this tragic possibility is indeed the crisis we face.

Made in the USA
Lexington, KY
29 February 2012